Editor
Eric Migliaccio

Managing Editor
Ina Massler Levin, M.A.

Illustrator
Tracy Reynolds

Cover Artist
Brenda DiAntonis

Art Manager
Kevin Barnes

Art Director
CJae Froshay

Imaging
James Edward Grace
Rosa C. See

Isabella

Publisher
Mary D. Smith, M.S. Ed.

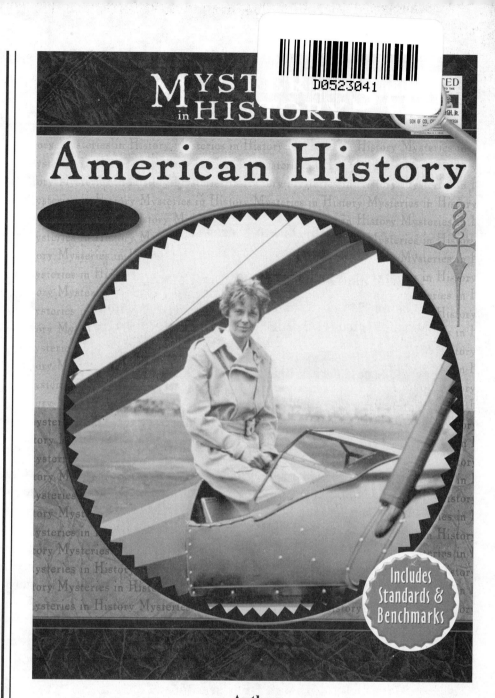

MYST in HISTORY
American History

Includes Standards & Benchmarks

Author

Wendy Conklin, M.A.

Teacher Created Resources

Teacher Created Resources, Inc.
6421 Industry Way
Westminster, CA 92683
www.teachercreated.com

ISBN: 978-1-4206-3047-3

©2005 Teacher Created Resources, Inc.
Reprinted, 2007
Made in U.S.A.

Table of Contents

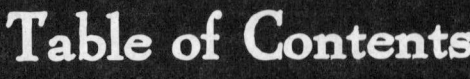

Why Study Mysteries?

What are the answers to the mysteries in American history? Was there a conspiracy to kill President Kennedy? What happened to Amelia Earhart? Were the Rosenbergs wrongly convicted? Who was responsible for the Lindbergh baby kidnapping? What caused the Salem witch trials? Who really discovered the Americas? What became of the lost colony at Roanoke? Who was involved in the Lincoln assassination conspiracy? What caused the *U.S.S. Maine* to explode? Will we ever really know the truth to these mysteries? Probably not—and that is precisely what makes these mysteries so useful to us today.

Why should we ask questions that cannot be answered with absolute certainty? Asking these types of questions demands that students speculate, debate, gather evidence, judge, evaluate, and compare. In this process, students use higher-level thinking skills. Their capacity to think critically increases with each new ambiguity. This book is designed to help students think critically. In addition, students also generate creative products, like journals, statements, verdicts, newspaper articles, tabloids, letters, cartoons, opinion polls, and profiles.

How This Book Is Organized

There are nine mysteries in this book. While the activities vary within each mystery, the layout for implementing the lessons is the same. Each mystery begins with an attention grabber. Some of these are in the form of a primary source (like diary entries and newspaper articles), and others are eye-catching posters and simulations. Students have the opportunity to discuss these attention grabbers. Each mystery also has a graphic organizer so that students can keep track of what they are learning. Every piece of background information needed for each mystery is provided in this unit. Teachers will not need to research beyond what is provided here. If students want to look into other aspects of the mysteries, resources are available in the bibliography at the end of the unit. The activities vary within each mystery. One has students put on a trial, another allows students to work for a newspaper, and yet another lets students work as investigators. Each mystery allows students to become the expert. They pull together pieces of information and make the final decision on the mystery, while providing evidence as support for their views.

Who Really Discovered the Americas?

Teacher Lesson Plan

Standard/Objective

* Students will demonstrate an understanding that different scholars may describe the same event or situation in different ways but must provide reasons or evidence for their views. (NCSS)

* Students will use evidence to support an explorer's claims and make final judgments regarding who discovered the Americas.

Materials

copies of *Attention Grabber* (page 8); copies of *Graphic Organizer* (page 9); copies of *Background Information* (pages 10–11); copies *A Documentary of Discovery* (pages 12–13); copies of *The Discovery Drawing* (page 14); for optional use, *Timeline of Events* (page 7)

Discussion Questions

* What does this quote mean?

* What is mysterious about this quote?

* Who do you think wrote this statement?

* Do you think the writer of this quote would have wanted others (for instance, us) to read this?

* Who discovered the Americas?

The Activity: Day 1

Begin this lesson by writing the following question on the board: "Who Discovered the Americas?" Have each student go up to the board and write his or her answer. Don't discuss their answers. Give each student a copy of the *Attention Grabber* (page 8). Give students enough time to analyze it and then ask the discussion questions above. For the last discussion question, refer to the answers written by the students on the board. Tell students that they will be researching their ideas and coming to a final conclusion on who really discovered the Americas.

Distribute a copy of *Graphic Organizer* (page 9) to each student. Have students write down the information that they know under the title "What I Know." Tell students to keep this graphic organizer in a safe place, because they will use it again as they record important information that they will learn.

Then distribute the *Background Information* (pages 10–11) and read it together as a class. Take time for students to ask and clarify questions as they read. Then have students take out their graphic organizers again and record notes about what they have learned under the title "What I Learned."

Teacher Lesson Plan *(cont.)*

The Activity: Day 2

Begin with this question: Who discovered the Americas? Have students look back at their notes on their graphic-organizer pages. Try to get students talking about this controversy. Tell students that they will be working in groups to produce a documentary for television. This documentary will explore the following question: Who discovered the Americas? Tell students that they will be presenting this documentary to the class. Divide students into three groups. Each group will represent one of the following: Christopher Columbus, the Vikings, or the Chinese. Tell each group that the goal of its members is to persuade their audience that their explorer reached the Americas first. Explain that it does not matter if they believe this is actually true. To accomplish this, each group will need to present facts that make their explorer look good. They can also use condemning evidence to show that the other two explorers did not reach the Americas first.

Distribute the student activity sheets *A Documentary of Discovery* (pages 12–13). Each student will have a job to do. Some will be writing questions to ask, and others will be preparing to answer those questions based on the evidence. Have students choose a part for their documentary. For example, there are three experts, one expert for each explorer: Columbus, Eriksson, and Zheng He. There are also interviewers. Each interviewer works on questions to ask the expert. Each expert prepares information to present on this documentary. Give each student time to work on their activity sheet individually.

The Activity: Day 3

Have each group consult together. For example, the group that represents Columbus should work together at this point. As a group they should compare notes for the documentary. As they compare notes, they should talk about the presentation and make adjustments to their presentation.

They also must decide on a format as a group. For example, will the documentary be a formal sit-down question-and-answer format? Or will it be broadcasting via satellite on location with each expert at the explorer's hometown? Have students discuss whether the public-opinion polls should be presented in the documentary. (This poll should be conducted as homework. Have students briefly present the evidence to family and friends outside of school.) Finally, give students time to practice their presentations.

Teacher Lesson Plan *(cont.)*

The Activity: Day 4

First, lead the entire class in creating a rubric for judging these documentaries. This can be done on the board or on an overhead projector. Categories can include presentation of each expert and interviewer, information presented, interesting format, convincing arguments, and overall performance of the crew. With the remaining time, have students practice their presentations. They should keep in mind how their documentaries will be performed live and judged by their peers on the following day.

The Activity: Day 5

Students will present their documentaries on this day. Give students some time to prepare.

It might be interesting to ask other staff members and classes to watch the presentations. If this is done, a poll should be taken both before and after the documentaries are shown. After each performance, distribute the rubric and let the audience judge the performance.

If available, use a video camera to tape the documentaries. Let students watch the presentations again. Ask the following questions:

* ❋ Who had the most convincing documentary?

* ❋ How much power does the media have over its viewers/readers/listeners?

* ❋ Do you think that most journalism is accurate? Why or why not?

* ❋ Is it possible to prove any viewpoint to viewers, regardless of what it is and its evidence?

Have students take out their graphic organizers. Each student should fill in the space titled "What I Still Want to Know." Then collect each student's graphic organizer. You should also collect the student activity sheets (pages 12–13).

Finally, distribute the student activity sheet titled *The Discovery Drawing* (page 14). Have students complete this page, recording their opinions on this mystery. If time permits, let students share their opinions in small groups.

Timeline of Events

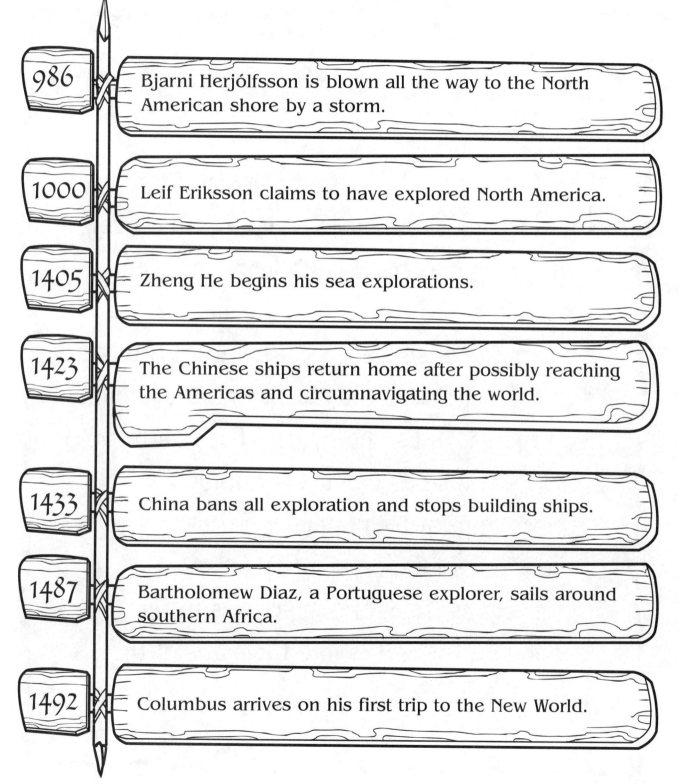

986 — Bjarni Herjólfsson is blown all the way to the North American shore by a storm.

1000 — Leif Eriksson claims to have explored North America.

1405 — Zheng He begins his sea explorations.

1423 — The Chinese ships return home after possibly reaching the Americas and circumnavigating the world.

1433 — China bans all exploration and stops building ships.

1487 — Bartholomew Diaz, a Portuguese explorer, sails around southern Africa.

1492 — Columbus arrives on his first trip to the New World.

Attention Grabber

Wednesday, October 24, 1492

...I have set sail for Cuba, which these natives have told me is very large and busy, with gold and spices, and large ships and merchants. They told me I could reach it by sailing west-southwest, which I think is true; for if this is the case, as all the Indians on these islands and those I have on board tell me (by signs because I cannot understand their language), I believe it to be the island of Cipango, of which such wonders are told, and which lies in this region on the globes and the maps of the world which I have seen...

Graphic Organizer

Directions: Who was the first to discover the Americas? Under the title "What I Know," write everything you know about this event. As you find out more information about this event, record your notes under the "What I Learned" title. After all of your research is complete, write your thoughts about this mystery under the title "What I Still Want to Know."

Background Information

Christopher Columbus

For many years, it was believed that the Italian Christopher Columbus was the first to reach the shores of the New World. He first asked the Portuguese King John II to support his exploration. Because money was tight, King John II refused. Columbus turned to Spain and asked King Ferdinand and Queen Isabella for help. They agreed and sent Columbus sailing west. Columbus landed in the Caribbean. His team explored parts of the Bahamas, including San Salvador, Cuba, Haiti, and the Dominican Republic (also called Hispaniola). Thinking he had reached the far eastern part of Asia known as the Indies, he called the natives Indians. Most history books credit Columbus as the first man to reach the Americas.

One disturbing fact has come to light from Columbus' log book. He makes a statement that seems to imply he knew he was not the first to reach the New World. He says, "I believe it to be the island of Cipango, of which such wonders are told, and which lies in this region on the globes and the maps of the world which I have seen…" If Columbus had a detailed and accurate map of the New World, where did he get such a map? How did the mapmakers know the area so well if they had never been there? Who gave the mapmakers that information?

The Vikings

The Vikings were people from Norway, Denmark, and Sweden. They invaded Europe and settled in new lands including Iceland and Greenland. In addition, the Vikings claim to have discovered, explored, and colonized North America before Columbus. Around 986, Viking Bjarni Herjólfsson was on a journey from Iceland to Greenland. He claims that a violent storm pushed his boat to the shores of North America. He did not stay to explore the area. Around 1000, Viking navigator Leif Eriksson claims to have explored the coasts of Labrador and Newfoundland. Because he saw so many grapes, he called the new land Vinland. In the past few years, it appears that old ruins have turned up in the area. This means that there was possibly a small village there.

In 1957, the Vinland map was discovered. It was a detailed map of Newfoundland and seemed to prove that the Vikings had arrived in the Americas at least 500 years before Columbus. The descriptions were consistent with the coast of Newfoundland, too. This map was created in the 1400s to commemorate the explorations of the Vikings.

However, as scholars have examined the map, some conflicting ideas have emerged. The carbon dating of the parchment paper dates it back to medieval times, which is consistent with the claim. So in other words, the paper was old, which was good. But there is disagreement on the ink that was used. Tests show that this ink has a chemical that was not used before the 1920s. Other tests show this chemical in very small traces in other medieval documents known to be authentic. A Norwegian historian even points to one man as the forger of this map. His name was Joseph Fischer, a German monk and medieval scholar. Why would he want to create a hoax? During the 1930s, the Nazi party used ancient Norse history as their propaganda. He may have opposed this exploitation. At this time, there is not enough ink on the map to use for radio carbon dating. It is hopeful that in the future a new way of dating the ink will be found and the controversy can be put to rest.

Background Information *(cont.)*

The Chinese

A man named Gavin Menzies believes that the Chinese were the first to land in the Americas and circumnavigate the globe. From 1405 to 1433, the Chinese led many expeditions to other countries. The construction of their boats was ahead of its time, and Zheng He was their chief explorer. His boats were 600 feet long with nine masts. (Columbus' largest ship, the *Santa Maria*, was only 98 feet long with three masts.) Their high-tech ships could store plenty of fresh water for the crew. They even grew gardens on the deck! About 1,000 men traveled on these expeditions, which could last up to three straight months without touching land.

Menzies believes that in 1421, Zheng He's fleet went around Africa's Cape of Good Hope and sailed west to Brazil. From there the ships went around the tip of South America. Some of the ships went toward Antarctica, others went up the west coast of the Americas to California, and some went back to China through the Pacific Ocean. Menzies claims that a few of the ships traveled to the Caribbean and eventually up the eastern coast of North America to Greenland and Iceland.

Menzies bases his theory on a few pieces of evidence. Chinese DNA has been found in the remains of people of the New World during that time. Both plants and animals indigenous to a particular continent have been found in both China and the New World. Finally—and most importantly to Menzies—he believes the remains of Chinese maps show that they explored the world. The Ryukoku map was drawn in Korea in about 1403. It was modified after 1420. It is a detailed map of the west coast of Africa. This has led many to believe that whoever explored the west coast of Africa had to have sailed around the Cape first. The Europeans had not begun their explorations before this time, so they could not have explored it. The Chinese Mao Kun map was created after Zheng He's expedition and it shows what looks like a Chinese ship at the tip of southern Africa. Only fragments of this map remain today.

Around the time of Zheng He's explorations, Europeans produced detailed maps. In particular, a Venetian mapmaker created a map called the Pizzigano Nautical Chart. It shows the coasts of Portugal, Spain, Africa, and what some think are the islands of Puerto Rico and Guadeloupe. What if the Chinese were the ones who explored this area first? How would the Europeans get the information from these Chinese explorers? Some think that Arab traders brought the information to the Europeans. Since the Arabs traveled from Venice to China regularly, they could have passed on the information. Unfortunately, written Chinese history will never tell, because all the records were destroyed when a new emperor came to power. They stopped building these amazing ships, and China turned its back on exploration.

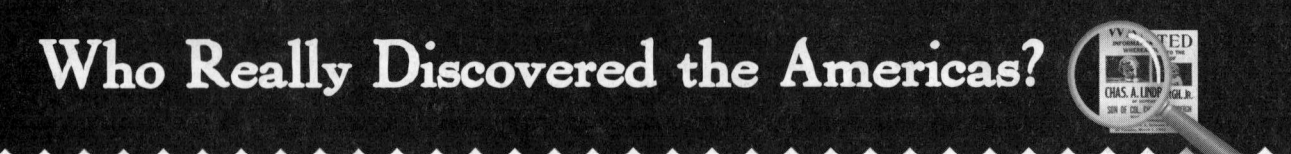

A Documentary of Discovery

Directions: Fill in the outline below to help you prepare for your documentary. Remember, it is your goal to prove that your explorer discovered the Americas first, regardless of what you personally believe. To do this, you will need to use the evidence wisely. How can you convince the audience that your explorer was first?

> **My group is preparing a documentary to prove that _____ discovered the Americas.**

Outline Preparation

I. List the strong points that should be covered in the documentary about your explorer.

_____

_____

_____

_____

_____

_____

II. List the condemning points that should be mentioned about the other explorers' claims.

_____

_____

_____

_____

_____

_____

A Documentary of Discovery *(cont.)*

III. You will need to conduct an outside opinion poll. How can your opinion poll support the evidence that you are trying to prove? Write questions for your opinion poll in the space below. Then present these questions to friends and family members and record their responses.

IV. Work in your group to decide on a format for your documentary. Brainstorm a list of ideas for your presentation on the web provided.

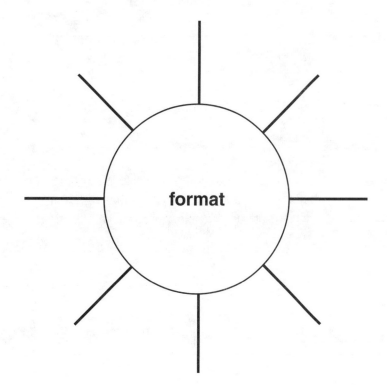

format

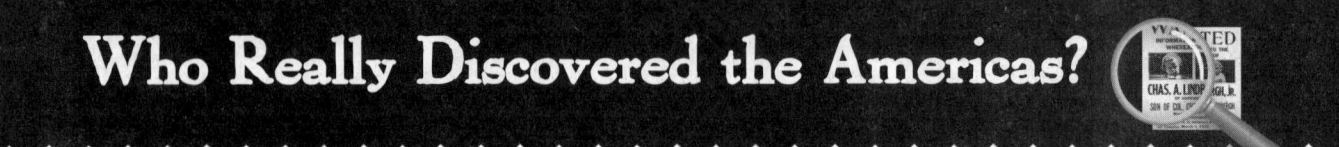

The Discovery Drawing

Directions: Who do you believe discovered the Americas? Why do you believe it? Is it based on the best evidence? In the space below, draw a picture that explains your answer to these questions. You can use words to label the picture.

What Happened to the Lost Colony?

Teacher Lesson Plan

Standard/Objective

- Students will explain how information and experiences may be interpreted by people from diverse cultural perspectives and frames of reference.
- Each student will create a story for either a tabloid or a news magazine that shows a solution to the mystery of the lost colony of Roanoke.

Materials

copies of *Attention Grabber* (page 18); copies of *Roanoke Map* (page 19); copies of *Graphic Organizer* (page 20); copies of *Background Information* (pages 21–23); copies of *Recipe for a Perfect Tabloid* and *Recipe for a Perfect News Magazine* (pages 24–25); copies of *The Tree Finally Speaks* (page 26); copies of actual tabloids and news magazines (see Teacher's Note on page 16)

Discussion Questions

- What do you think John White was writing about?
- What do you think CRO stands for?
- In what ways does this evidence solve the mystery?
- In what ways does this evidence make this a mystery?

The Activity: Day 1

Attention Grabber

Make several copies of *Attention Grabber* (page 18), enough for each student in the class and a few extras. On the extra copies, cut off John White's journal entry at the bottom and throw it away. Before students come to class, hang these copies of the tree trunk around the room in various places so that students will see them. Don't provide students with any answers. After students have become quite curious, distribute a copy of the attention grabber (including the bottom quote from John White) to each student. Read it aloud as a class and ask the discussion questions above. Tell students that even when the answer to a mystery seems to be quite obvious, there could be other answers to it. Tell students that this quote is about the lost colony of Roanoke. This colony was settled 37 years before the Pilgrims arrived in America. There were over 100 men, women, and children in this colony. Distribute the *Roanoke Map* (page 19) and let students see where Roanoke is located.

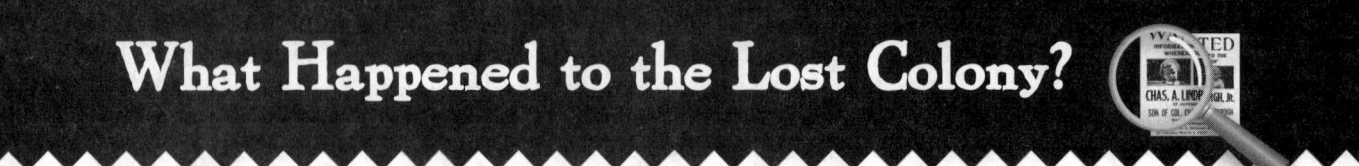

Teacher Lesson Plan *(cont.)*

The Activity: Day 1 *(cont.)*

Distribute *Graphic Organizer* (page 20) to each student. Have students write down the information that they know under the title "What I Know." Tell students to keep this graphic organizer in a safe place, because they will use it again as they record important information that they will learn.

Distribute copies of *Background Information* (pages 21–23) and have students read it together in small groups. Bring students back as a class and take time for students to ask and clarify questions. Then have students take out their graphic organizers again and, under the title "What I Learned," have students record notes about what they have learned.

The Activity: Day 2

Put this question on the board: "What happened to the Lost Colony?" Have students look back at their notes on their graphic-organizer pages. Try to get students talking about this controversy. Tell students that they will choose a view and write a news story about it. This view does not necessarily have to be their personal view.

Their solution to the mystery of the lost colony of Roanoke will be written in a news story in one of two formats: tabloid or news magazine. It would be helpful to bring in a copy of both of these so that students can get a first-hand look at the types of stories that each one has printed.

> **Teacher's Note:** *It should be noted that tabloid newspapers or news magazines could have inappropriate stories, so teachers should preview the printed materials and censor some of the stories by tearing them out.*

Write "Tabloid" on one small sheet of paper and write "News Magazine" on another small sheet of paper. Put these two papers in a hat. Have each student draw one of these papers out of a hat. This will be the format by which that student will write his/her story. Distribute *Recipe for a Perfect Tabloid* or *Recipe for a Perfect News Magazine* (pages 24–25), depending on which story each student will write. This activity sheet will help students organize their news stories. Let students spend the remaining time organizing the points of their stories.

The Activity: Day 3

Tell students that they will begin writing their stories today. Have them use information on their graphic organizers, background information, and student activity sheets to help them write. Each story should be at least one page in length and have at least one picture.

Teacher Lesson Plan *(cont.)*

The Activity: Day 4

Let students finish writing their stories. Before turning in their stories, let students share them with the class. These would also make a great display on a bulletin board.

Ask the following questions:

* ✳ Who had the most convincing story? What made it convincing?

* ✳ How much power does the printed material have over its readers?

* ✳ How does the type of paper (tabloid, magazine) affect how a story is reported?

* ✳ Which type of printed material (tabloid, magazine) do you think is most reliable?

* ✳ Is it fair to categorize the type of person who buys a tabloid or a news magazine? Why or why not?

Have students take out their graphic organizers. Each student should fill in the space titled "What I Still Want to Know." Then collect each student's graphic organizer. You should also collect the student activity sheets.

The Activity: Day 5

Finally, distribute the student activity sheet *The Tree Finally Speaks* (page 26). Students will be using this page to write their opinions about what happened to the colonists on Roanoke Island. Students will be writing their opinions of what happened to the Lost Colony from the tree's perspective. In addition to making students use higher-level thinking skills as they make judgments, this activity also allows students to use their creativity as they make the tree tell the "true" story. If time permits, let students share their stories in small groups. As an added extension, have students dress up as trees and present their stories to the class the following day.

Attention Grabber

...As we went inshore up the sandy bank we saw a tree on the brow of a cliff curiously carved with the clear Roman letters CRO. We knew at once that these letters indicated the place to which the planters had gone. Before I left them we had agreed on a secret token. They were to write or carve on trees or doorposts the name of the place where they had settled...

— John White, 1590

Roanoke Map

ROANOKE
ISLAND

VIRGINIA

ATLANTIC
OCEAN

NORTH
CAROLINA

Graphic Organizer

Directions: What happened to the Lost Colony of Roanoke? Under the title "What I Know," write everything you know about this event. As you find out more information about this event, record your notes under the "What I Learned" title. After all your research is complete, write everything else you would like to know under the title "What I Still Want to Know."

What I Know

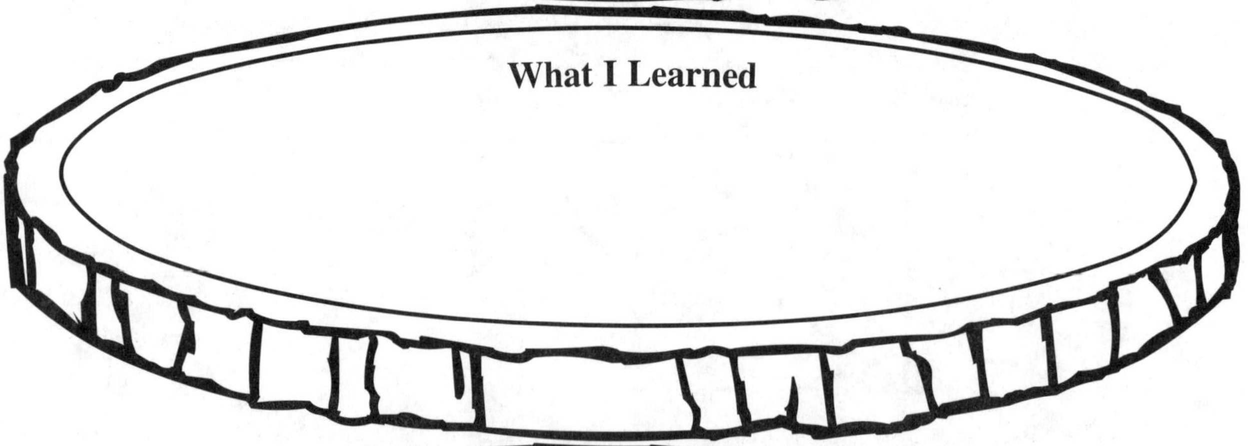

What I Learned

What I Still Want to Know

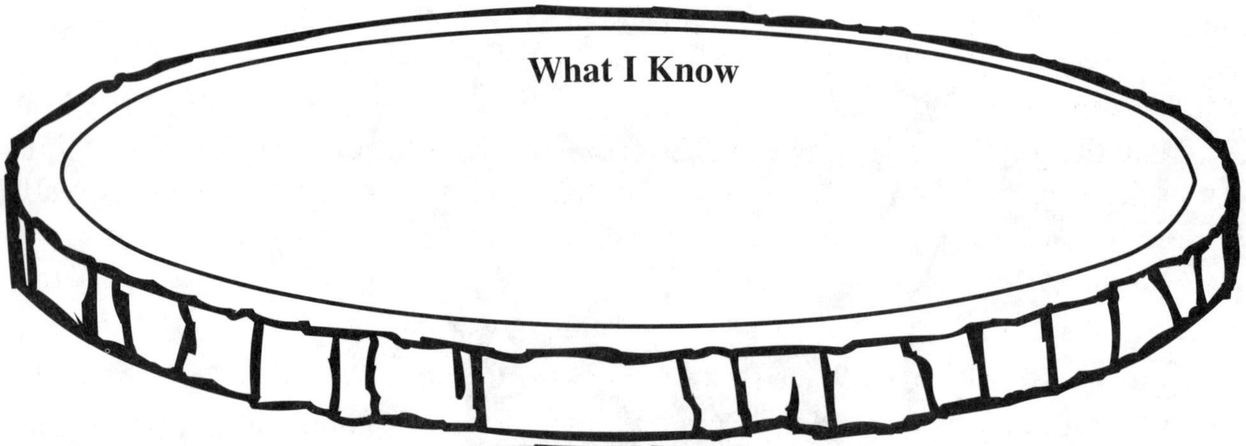

What Happened to the Lost Colony?

Background Information

About 37 years before the Pilgrims landed at Plymouth Rock, the first colony was established in the New World. It was the colony at Roanoke.

Sir Walter Raleigh, an English explorer and writer, had an interest in helping England colonize the New World. In 1584, Raleigh paid two English navigators to explore the possibility of setting up a colony in the New World. These navigators were Philip Amadas and Arthur Barlowe. They found an island right off the coast of North Carolina. Within days these explorers met with friendly American Indians. Amadas and Barlowe noticed that the ground seemed fertile and recommended it for colonization. They took two American Indians, Wanchese and Manteo, back to England. The expedition greatly impressed both Raleigh and the queen and they named the land Virginia in honor of the "Virgin Queen." Queen Elizabeth I gave a grant for the land, and the next year more than 100 men set sail with Raleigh's cousin, Sir Richard Grenville.

The American Indians on Roanoke Island welcomed the men. A spot at the north end of the island was chosen and the men began building a fort and cottage-like homes using bricks and thatched roofs. Grenville returned to England to tell of their success and to get more supplies. Ralph Lane was appointed governor and left in charge of the colony.

Unknown to Grenville, these new settlers soon faced serious problems. To begin with, the men landed too late to plant crops. They had to rely on the American Indians for food. Friendships with the American Indians became strained when the settlers kidnapped them in exchange for information. In return, the settlers' fish traps were repeatedly robbed or destroyed. In desperation, groups of men were sent to the shore to search for seafood and ships. By the beginning of June, the settlers were at war with the American Indians, and some American Indians died in the conflicts.

Unfortunately, Grenville's trip back to the colony was delayed. The settlers were desperate. On June 9, word was brought to Lane that Sir Francis Drake was on the coast with 23 ships. Drake offered a ship filled with supplies to Lane. Lane was told that he and the men could take this ship back to England in a month, or they could return immediately with Drake himself. Lane hated the idea of giving up this colony, but he realized that his men were in desperate need and could no longer survive. He agreed to take the ship and sail back a month later. In the meantime, the ship was blown out to sea in a terrible storm. It did not return. Drake offered him another ship, but Lane and his men decided to sail immediately with Drake. On June 18, all of the colonists set sail for England.

more to follow

Background Information *(cont.)*

A short while later, Grenville arrived back at the colony with three loaded ships. He searched in vain for the settlers and decided to leave 15 men behind to keep the land for England. He left the men with enough supplies to last two full years.

In 1587, Raleigh decided to set up another settlement. This time he sent several families, including women and children. He also appointed John White to be the governor. The settlers intended to go to the Chesapeake Bay area, thinking it would be a better place to settle. On their way, the crew stopped at the island to pick up the 15 men who were left behind by Grenville. No one was found except the remains of one man, obviously slaughtered by the American Indians. The cottage-like houses were still standing, but the fort had been destroyed completely. The crew assumed that all the men had been killed.

Perhaps because it was already late in the season (July), White decided to stay in the old settlement instead of pushing on to the Chesapeake Bay area. Not long after, one of the men was found murdered, presumably by the Roanoke Island Indians (also called Roanokes). Manteo relayed the information that the Roanokes lived in a village on the mainland, and so the Englishmen formed a raiding party and attacked the village. After the attack, the Englishmen discovered that the Roanokes had already fled and the victims in the village were the friendly Croatoans, who were gathering the spoils. At the time, Manteo was able to patch up this misunderstanding between the English and the Croatoans. It is unknown for sure whether the Croatoans actually forgave the settlers.

At the end of August, Governor White left for England to gather more supplies. Before he had left, he devised a code for the settlers to use if they had to leave the island. They were to pick a tree and carve on it the destination where they were going. If they were in distress, they were to carve a Maltese cross over the destination. Unfortunately, White left at a bad time. Upon arriving back in England, a war had broken out between the English and the Spanish. All of the ships were needed for battle. For over two years, the settlers had no contact with White or England.

more to follow

Background Information *(cont.)*

Finally, in 1590, White was able to sail back. When he arrived at the settlement, he noticed that the homes had been torn down. The village had been heavily fenced with large trees so that it looked like a fort. White noticed that the letters "CRO" had been carved on one of the trees. On one of the fence posts the word "Croatoan" had been carved, but there was not a Maltese cross. White assumed that the settlers had gone to the Croatoan Island. He and the crew made their way back to the ship and planned to go to the island the next day. Unfortunately, a terrible storm kept them from the island, so they tried to sail to the West Indies for supplies. Instead of landing, a hurricane blew them out to sea, and they were forced to sail back to England. White was never again able to raise money to travel to America.

So what happened to the colony of Roanoke, which consisted of more than 100 men, women, and children? In the summer of 1588, the Spanish had sent a scouting party to Roanoke. They did not report any findings. In other words, they did not see any people or remains of people. In 1607, Jamestown was established. An American Indian chief there boasted of killing the Roanoke colonists. In 1709, John Lawson spent time exploring an area inhabited by descendants of the Croatoan tribe. He claimed that many of the natives were white people. He also said that some of them had gray eyes, something not heard of among the American Indians. In the 1880s, it was noted by a man living in southeastern North Carolina that the American Indians there looked very European, with fair skin and light hair and eyes. In 1998 archaeologists analyzed the tree rings where the colony once stood. The tree rings seem to suggest that there was a severe drought in the area around 1587. In fact, it was the worst drought in 800 years! This would have caused food to be in short supply, too.

All this evidence suggests a few ideas: either the neighboring American Indians killed the settlers; or the settlers died from a drought; or they assimilated into a tribe, possibly on the Croatoan Island. Maybe there are other possibilities. Only the island knows the truth—and it's not talking!

Recipe for a Perfect Tabloid

Directions: Many people tune in to the news each day to find out what is going on in the world. What if television did not exist? How would people get their news? Most likely it would have to be written news. You will be creating a story about one theory of the Lost Colony of Roanoke. Your story will be published in a tabloid paper. Fill in the information below to help you organize your story.

Recipe for a Perfect Tabloid

* Scandalous or Incriminating Pictures
* Flashy Title
* Content Blown Out of Proportion
* Must Have Some Kernel of Truth

Name of my tabloid: _____

Title of my story: _____

Theory on the reasons for the Lost Colony: _____

_____

What kind of picture will I use? _____

What content will be blown out of proportion? _____

Describe the kind of person that would be interested in reading this story.

_____

_____

_____

What information will you use to make your readers draw a certain conclusion?

_____

_____

_____

_____

Recipe for a Perfect News Magazine

Directions: Many people tune into the news each day to find out what is going on in the world. What if television did not exist? How would people get their news? Most likely it would have to be written news. You will be creating a story about one theory of the Lost Colony of Roanoke. Your story will be published in a news magazine. Fill in the information below to help you organize your story.

Recipe for a Perfect News Magazine

* Catchy Title

* Interesting Pictures

* Exclusive Interviews

* Accurate Information

Name of my news magazine: _____

Title of my story: _____

Theory on the reasons for the Lost Colony: _____

_____

What kind of picture will I use?_____

Who will be featured in an exclusive interview? _____

Describe the kind of person that would be interested in reading this story.

_____

_____

What information will you use to make your readers draw a certain conclusion?

_____

_____

_____

_____

_____

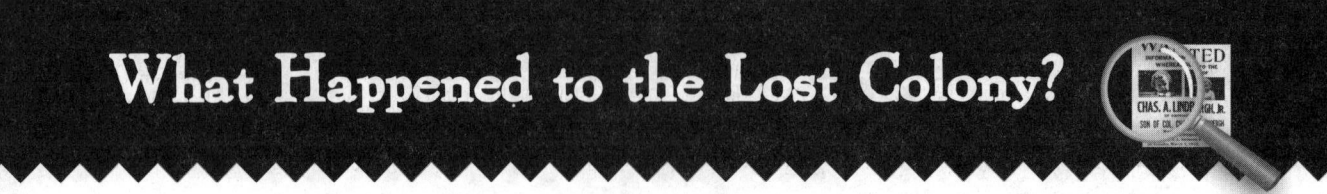
The Tree Finally Speaks

Directions: What do you believe happened to the Lost Colony of Roanoke? Why do you believe it? Is it based on the best evidence? Only the island itself really knows. Pretend you are the tree with the "CRO" carved on it. You know what happened. As the tree, tell your story in the space below.

_____

_____

_____

_____

_____

_____

_____

_____

_____

_____

_____

_____

_____

_____

_____

_____

The Salem Witch Trials

Teacher Lesson Plans

Standard/Objective

✳ Develop critical sensitivities such as empathy and skepticism regarding attitudes, values, and behaviors of people in different historical contexts. (NCSS)

✳ Students will examine trial testimony and other background information and then write a statement from an accuser that explains the mystery of the Salem accusations and outbursts.

Materials

copies of *Attention Grabber* (pages 30–32); copies of *Folk Magic* (page 33); copies of *Background Information* (pages 34–36); copies of *Graphic Organizer* (page 37); copies of *Tituba's Trial* (pages 38–40); copies of *Rebecca Nurse's Trial* (pages 41–43); copies of *A Statement from Ann* (page 44); various fairytale books that include witches (e.g., *Sleeping Beauty*, *Snow White*)

> **Teacher's Note:** *Be aware that some students might have difficulty with this topic. Please review it before teaching it to your class.*

Discussion Questions

✳ How did this simulation make you feel?

✳ Do you think these witch trials were fair?

✳ What do you know about the Salem witch trials?

✳ How do you think people discovered if someone was a witch or not?

The Activity: Day 1

To set the mood, you might want to wear a long black cape and maybe even a witch's hat. Darken the lights in the room. Tell students to close their eyes and listen to the story that you are about to tell them. Read the *Attention Grabber* (pages 30–32) visualization aloud to the class. When you get to the part that asks students what they will do, have the two sections at the end ready to distribute to students. Students who choose to admit that they are witches will get #1; students who choose to continue to profess their innocence will get #2. Tell students to open their eyes and read their chosen sections quietly to themselves. Then ask the discussion questions above.

Teacher Lesson Plans *(cont.)*

The Activity: Day 1 *(cont.)*

Make a list of students' ideas for the last question. Then distribute copies of *Folk Magic* (page 33). This page gives a list of ways that witches were "detected," as well as popular forms of folk magic that were used back during colonial times. Be sure to explain that "witches" during that time were not the same as "witches" are today. There is a difference between what we see as the modern practice of Wicca and the witches during the colonial period. A witch during colonial times was someone who used magic to hurt others.

Distribute copies of the *Background Information* (pages 34–36). Before students read, make a point of telling students that one major character in the Salem Witch Trials was a woman named Tituba. She is referred to as an Indian, not as a Native American or an American Indian, because she is from the Caribbean. Have students read this information with a partner. Then bring the class back together. Ask students to think about living in a society where an accusation makes one guilty of a crime. Why would someone accuse an innocent person and what caused the outbursts in Salem? Tell students that they will be working on this very mystery about the Salem Witch Trials for the week.

The Activity: Day 2

Bring in copies of various fairytale books that contain the character of a witch and display them in front of the room. Divide students into groups and give each group a book to read aloud. One person in the group can be the designated reader, or students can take turns reading the books. Tell students to make a group list of the characteristics of the witch as the story is read. If time permits, let students read the entire story.

Bring the class back together again and let each group present their list of characteristics to the class. See if there are similarities. Then have students reflect back on the background information concerning Salem and the witch trials. How can Salem be compared to a fairytale? What did the people (or the students) want to happen to the witch in the story? Many times they (and the students) wanted her dead. This was similar to what the people wanted in Salem.

Ask students to look at the story from the witch's point of view. Why was she an angry old woman? Was she owed something? Did society or the "good guys" slight her? Explain to students that these fairytales were much like life back during the times of the Salem witch trials. Woman who did not fit in with society were sometimes slighted as witches. If women spoke out, if they did not have children, or if they were bitter against society, then they were an easy target for this accusation.

Distribute the *Graphic Organizer* (page 37). Have students record their ideas of the many different motives for accusing someone of being a witch in Salem. Students will want to keep this organizer and add to it as they read through the trial transcripts during the following days.

Teacher Lesson Plans *(cont.)*

The Activity: Day 3

Ask students what they think these trials were like. Tell students that they will be reading the transcripts of a trial today. This transcript shows the trial of an Indian woman named Tituba. She was a slave taken from Barbados in the Caribbean, and she served in the home of the Salem Village minister, Samuel Parris. Remind students that the Indian people were always under suspicion in the colonies. Distribute copies of *Tituba's Trial* (pages 38–40). This transcript is a paraphrased modern translation of what the trial was like. Assign parts to the students and let them read it aloud. Then let students discuss what they read as a class. One discussion question might be, "Why would Tituba admit to being a witch if she really was not one?" Again, give students time to add any information to their graphic organizers.

The Activity: Day 4

Explain to students that they will be reading another trial transcript today. This time, the accused woman, Rebecca Nurse, was an upstanding woman in Salem. Distribute copies of *Rebecca Nurse's Trial* (pages 41–43). Assign parts and let students read the transcripts aloud. Allow time for students to talk about her trial. One discussion question might be, "Why would the jury change its mind about her innocence?" Again, give students a moment to add any final thoughts to their graphic organizers.

The Activity: Day 5

Distribute copies of *A Statement from Ann* (page 44). For this activity, students will be writing a letter to the church in Salem. This letter should explain why the innocent people were accused and what caused the outbursts in Salem. Be sure to tell students that this letter will be read aloud to the church. Acting as the minister of Salem Village, read these statements aloud to the class. If time permits, let students research to find out what Ann actually said to her church members.

Attention Grabber

The long, dusty walk from Salem Town will do you some good on this humid afternoon. You feel extra hot under the skin because you've been haggling with the wealthy merchants in town. They charge exorbitant prices, much too high for you to pay. They offer no sympathy for you, a poor farmer in Salem Village. You catch yourself wishing evil on them, but then remember that thoughts like those come from the Devil. You know you must forgive that money-grabbing merchant, but find it very difficult to do. You quickly ask for forgiveness and leave those thoughts behind you.

You carefully place one foot in front of the other on the rough road. This trip seems extra long. Your thirst makes you think of stopping at the public house for some refreshing cider. You can see the small pub in the distance. It looks rustic and quite cozy on this hazy afternoon. You know while you are there that you will probably hear some more of those witch tales. Maybe even some of those accusers, the young girls, will be there.

You walk inside, brushing your hands gently against the crude wooden doors. Ouch! A small splinter slides into your palm. Your eyes adjust to the dark room. Candles and lanterns dimly light the place. You find a private place to sit. You can see everyone from this position. Some are laughing, others look tired, as you do. Many are neighbors you've known all your life. Your mind begins to wonder about what the pastor said last Sunday: "Satan is loose in Salem. He is disguised among you." As you look around, you ask yourself who of these neighbors could be disguised as a witch? Could he be a witch? Is she a witch? Already Tituba, the slave girl, has confessed to being a witch. She has named others who have signed the Devil's book. It won't stop with just her. The evil must be purged from Salem.

Ann Putnam, a 12-year-old, is in the center of the room. Her friend Abigail Williams is there, too. They appear to be so confident, and at this moment they seem perfectly normal to you. Secretly you were hoping to see them in one of their fits. In a strange way, these evil outbursts seem so fascinating.

Abigail notices you staring at her. You look away, embarrassed, wondering if she could read your thoughts. Suddenly her eyes widen and her body begins convulsing. Then Ann's body goes limp and she slumps to the floor. They both shake and scream. Then Abigail spreads her arms and moves about as if she is flying around the room. She lets out a blood-curdling sound more like a chicken squawk than a dog's bark.

Attention Grabber *(cont.)*

People there begin asking her, "Who torments you, Abigail? Who is doing this to you? Tell us, Abigail! Tell us!" All the while she yells and runs. She quiets for only a moment, then names her torturer: you!

You awake to find the chains wrapped about your body. The damp, musty smell of the cell no longer bothers you. The girls claim that your ghost torments them in their homes. To keep your ghost in the cell, the jailer has placed heavy irons about your feet. You can barely move.

You look around the cell and see Sarah Osborne. You know that she is a witch. You attended her trial. You remember seeing her puppets that she stuck pins into hoping to hurt those children. She deserves to hang. It was God's judgment. You see Rebecca Nurse and can't believe that she's a witch. She prays in church. You've seen her there every Sunday, rain or shine.

Your trial takes place where all the others have, in the familiar church that you have attended ever since moving to Salem. You long to sit on your familiar pew, but instead you are taken to the front of the crowded room. You stand before them as the crowd waits in anticipation. One by one, you hear harsh words muttered by all of your neighbors. They all have suspected that you were a witch. Everyone watches you closely as the girls testify how you have tormented them. Every move you make seems to cause pain in some way to them. If you scratch your arm, they cry out that you are pinching them. If you turn around, they say you are trying to break their necks. Some say they saw you turn into a bird and fly away from a house in the village. Others show teeth marks that they claim have come from you. Another young girl screams that your ghost just stabbed her. She holds up the end of a knife as her proof. The judges are impressed and look at you in a condemning way. A boy in the audience claims that the knife belongs to him. He threw it away in a trash heap as he passed by the girl's house last evening. The judges look at the girl and warn her to never lie again to the court. They are satisfied when the girl agrees.

The questions are thrown to you now: "Are you a witch? Why do you hurt these children? How can you be sure that you are not a witch? We know that you are a witch. Confess! How long have you been a witch? Confess! How long have you been an instrument of the Devil? When did you sign his red book? Confess!"

✳ How will you answer?

✳ Will you admit to being a witch?

✳ Will you continue to profess your innocence?

Attention Grabber *(cont.)*

1. *You admit to being a witch.*

You begin thinking, "Maybe I really am a witch. I've thought some terrible thoughts about those merchants in Salem Town. I even played around with some old folk magic, like looking at egg whites in water to see the future."

You spend a year in the damp, cold cell with the other professed witches. You are needed to keep the cases going in Salem. You have to point out other witches in the community. You struggle with betraying innocent people. At the end of that time, the English governor pardons you. You walk into your house and find everything in shambles. It's very dusty and has been abandoned by your family.

You know that before this all started you were a devout member of the church. You prayed every day. You thought your faith was sincere. Yes, it was sincere. What is it now that you have betrayed innocent blood? Yes, you have saved your life, but you have lost your soul in the process.

- -

2. *You continue to profess your innocence.*

You find yourself back in the damp musty cell. You will await your trial. Will you be declared innocent? Up to this point, all have been convicted.

After a few months your trial begins. You are relieved to get out of the cell for a few hours a day. One by one the girls testify about how you have hurt them. You struggle to show that you are a person, an upstanding godly person. You can only hope that the jury sees you for who you are. They leave to deliberate the case. They return with a "Not Guilty" verdict. You are so relieved, and nearly pass out at the announcement. The courtroom erupts in anger and screams from the tormented accusers. The jury is told to go back and rethink the case one more time. They return with a verdict of "Guilty." You go back to jail to await your hanging.

Folk Magic

Directions: There were many ways to tell a witch from a regular person. Here are some descriptions of what New Englanders thought at the time and some common folk magic practiced by many.

The Rye Cake Test

Mix the afflicted girl's urine with rye flour and bake it into a biscuit. Feed it to a dog. The animal will either say the name of the witch responsible for hurting the girl, or the animal will lead the others to the witch. The witch might even be drawn to the animal.

The Puritans brought this test over from England.

If Tituba did perform this test, she learned it from her English neighbors and masters.

The Lord's Prayer

If a person could say the Lord's Prayer without mistake, he or she could be cleared of being a witch. It was believed that a witch could not say the Lord's Prayer.

Foretelling the Future

Drop an egg white in water. Wait to see what shapes form. These shapes will foretell the future. Another test was dropping nails into grease. The patterns left by the nails could foretell the future.

Through the Tree

If children were pressed through a hole in a natural object, then they would be immune to witchcraft. There was a hole in a tree in Salem. It was just the right size for an infant to pass through. Parents continued passing their children through that hole until 1793.

Iron

Iron found in horseshoes was supposed to keep witches away from a house. Many hung these on the doorway to their homes.

Healing

Rhymes were said to heal toothaches, fevers, warts, and wounds.

Balancing Act

Sieves were balanced between two scissor blades. Bibles were bound together with string and a key placed in the middle, as if it were a bookmark. Two people (one on each side) balanced these items with one finger. Any twitches were interpreted as answering their questions.

Searching the Body

A suspected witch's body was searched for any unusual mole or mark. These marks usually meant she was indeed a witch.

Background Information

Phoebe Chandler, a 12-year-old girl, was sent out by her mother to fetch beer for some thirsty workers. As she walked to get it, a voice came out from the bushes and asked her what she was doing and where she was going. Phoebe thought the voice sounded like Martha Carrier, a grouchy neighbor in the town. She looked around and saw no one. Scared, she ran fast to get away from there. A few hours later, Phoebe's mother sent her out to do another chore. As she walked, she heard the same voice. The voice told her that in a few days she would be poisoned. Within a few days, her arm had swollen and was in a great deal of pain. Was this merely a coincidence? Another man in town had a real-life encounter with Martha Carrier. They argued over some land, and it seemed to this man that Carrier put a curse on him. Within days he suffered from a swollen foot and sores. When Carrier was arrested, these ailments went away. Was Martha Carrier a witch? Did she have magical power to hurt her neighbors?

While not everyone believed in witches during colonial times, there were some who definitely did believe. The Puritan church believed in the supernatural. They believed that if there was a God, there was also a Devil who actively roamed about. Throughout New England, various people were accused of being witches. Many of these cases were brought to trial. But these cases were hard to prove and many of the judges ruled against the accusers. Many places in Europe allowed the accusers to torture the defendants in hopes of getting the truth out of them. A popular test in England was to dunk the defendant under water to see if she would float. A real witch, according to the court, would float. These types of tests were banned entirely in New England. It was harder to get the evidence needed in the colonies because it was against the law to torture the defendants. What sets Salem apart from the other colonies is that the Salem courts convicted and hanged 19 people. The courts in Salem really believed that the accused were witches.

What would drive people to accuse their neighbors of being witches? Could these people have really been witches? Or did some get accused because of jealousy or vengeance? What caused the accusers' strange outbursts? Did the young accusers like getting attention? Did they feel guilty for dabbling in some folk magic? Did they see something that scared them while using a little folk magic? Because people's motives cannot be known, we can only speculate.

more to follow

Background Information *(cont.)*

In 1688, just four years before the Salem incident, a Boston family by the name of Goodwin struggled with their children. These children began acting out in strange ways. A doctor was called to evaluate the children. He came to the conclusion that the children were suffering from witchcraft. The maid was blamed for bewitching the four children. A famous minister named Cotton Mather arrived at the home in hopes of helping these afflicted children. The maid was brought to trial, convicted, and hanged. Mather wrote a book on his experience with the Goodwin children. It was widely read in the colonies, especially by young people.

Folk magic was big among the colonists. Many colonists used astrological charts to tell the future. Some carried charms for good luck, while others used rituals to help them interpret God's will. Some of these colonists were members of the Puritan church. Week after week the minister of the church would condemn the use of these evil things. Was it possible that some of the young girls might have dabbled in these practices as a form of rebellion against their Puritanistic families and felt guilty?

Salem, Massachusetts, was a small town established by the Puritans in the 1600s. The Puritans saw themselves in combat with the world. If it was not the neighboring tribe of Indians, then it was the Devil. The town of Salem was sharply divided. The Puritans wanted to protect their simple way of life; the merchants wanted to expand their way of life in Salem. Salem soon split into two towns: Salem Town, where the merchants lived, and Salem Village, where the Puritans lived. Conflicts arose from inheritance battles over land. Courts ruled in favor of the wealthy merchants. There were many families affected by these decisions in the Puritan church. No doubt that the children from these afflicted homes heard about these conflicts and how their families had been slighted. Could the trials have stemmed from vengeance or jealousy?

more to follow

Background Information (cont.)

A minister named Samuel Parris was elected to serve the Puritan church in Salem Village. He had previously tried to prosper as a Salem Town merchant, but failed. (Could he have been just as bitter as many of the families in the Puritan church?) The people in Salem believed he was just the right minister for them. Parris had a nine-year-old daughter and 12-year-old niece. Early in 1692, they suddenly started behaving strangely. It was reported that they were pinched and bitten by something invisible. Their bodies convulsed and twisted in unnatural positions. They appeared to be tormented by something unseen. Other people were more skeptical. They reported that these girls crawled under chairs and into holes. They muttered silly speeches that made them look ridiculous. Both the skeptic and the believer did agree on one key point: these girls were experiencing the same thing as the Goodwin children experienced. Did these girls read Mather's book? Were they good at mimicking? Or was something sinister invisibly lurking in the town?

Their afflictions were contagious—but only those living in Salem Village, not Salem Town, were affected. Some began suffering from bites, pinches, and disturbing fits. The skeptics said they were good at drama. At the center of the fits or drama were several young ladies. They were a 12-year-old named Ann Putnam, her mother, their servant named Mercy Lewis, a relative named Mary Walcott, a physician's niece named Elizabeth Hubbard, and a 22-year-old servant named Mary Warren. Instead of questioning, "What did I do that allowed the devil to torment me?" they began asking, "Who is using the devil against me?"

Parris had a slave from the Caribbean named Tituba. She was an Indian woman. The colonists had bad feelings toward the Indians already. Was it possible that they wanted to make this Indian woman the scapegoat for these troubled feelings? The tormented girls named Tituba as the source of their torment. They named Sarah Good, too. She was a poor woman in her late 30s who was not well-liked by the community. Even her husband claimed that she was a witch. They also labeled Sarah Osborne, a woman who was caught living with a man after her husband died and had skipped church for more than a year. The tormented girls could not have picked a better assortment of witches: an Indian, a woman no one liked, and a woman whom people gossiped about. These were just the types of people many believed were witches. On February 29, the law stepped in and brought these three women to a pretrial hearing. From this point on, the crisis in Salem escalated, until 19 people (including both men and women) were hanged for witchcraft.

Graphic Organizer

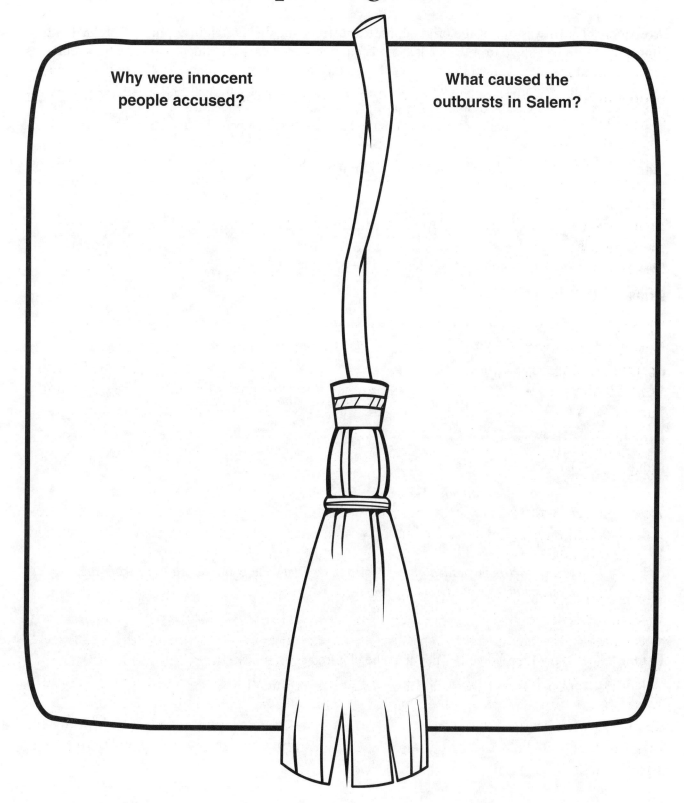

Why were innocent
people accused?

What caused the
outbursts in Salem?

Tituba's Trial

Directions: Tituba was one of the original three accused of being a witch in Salem Village in 1692. Tituba was an Indian slave from Barbados, a place in the Caribbean. The local minister, Samuel Parris, owned her. Tituba first claimed to be innocent, but during this final examination she admitted to being a witch—and named other women, too. One account from the time said that Parris had beaten Tituba until she confessed and named others. Most of this account is a modern translation taken from the actual trial transcript, but it also adds in what many have reported happened in the courtroom, as well.

Judge Tituba, what evil spirits are you familiar with?

Tituba No evil spirits.

    (Ann cries out in anguish, as if Tituba were hurting her.)

Judge Why do you hurt these children that are accusing you?

Tituba I don't hurt them.

    (As Tituba glances toward the girls, the girls fall down on the floor, as if in a spell. Mercy Lewis suddenly cries out in pain.)

Judge Then who hurts them?

    (Mary Walcott yells out that she sees a ghost hovering above Tituba.)

Tituba The Devil, for all I know.

Judge Did you ever see the Devil?

    (Tituba glances toward her owner, Reverend Parris, and then suddenly changes her story.)

Tituba Yes, the Devil came to me and asked me to serve him.

    (The courtroom suddenly gets very quiet. Everyone is interested in hearing this confession, especially the accusers.)

Judge Who else have you seen?

Tituba I saw four women. They hurt the children sometimes.

    (Ann's mother cries out, "Yes! They have hurt us!")

Tituba's Trial *(cont.)*

Judge   Who were these women?

Tituba   I saw Sarah Osborne and Sarah Good. I don't know the other woman. Both Sarah Osborne and Sarah Good wanted me to hurt the children, but I would not do it. There was a tall man from Boston there, too.

Judge   When did you see them last?

Tituba   Last night in Boston.

Judge   What did they say to you?

Tituba   They said to hurt the children.

Judge   Did you hurt them?

Tituba   They hurt the children, and then they threatened to hurt me if I did not hurt the children.

Judge   But didn't you hurt the children, too?

Tituba   Yes, I did. But I will not hurt them anymore.

Judge   Are you sorry for hurting them?

Tituba   Yes, I am very sorry.

Judge   Describe what you saw.

Tituba   A man came to me and told me to serve him.

Judge   What did he want you to do?

Tituba   He told me to kill the children last night. He said that if I would not do this, they would do worse to me.

Judge   What does he look like?

Tituba   Sometimes he looks like a hog. Other times he looks like a great dog.

Judge   What did you tell him?

Tituba   I said that if I would hurt them, he would give me many pretty things. He had a pretty yellow bird with him.

(Elizabeth cries that the bird is sitting on Tituba's shoulder.)

Tituba's Trial *(cont.)*

Judge	What else did you see?
Tituba	Two rats. One was red, and the other was black.
Judge	Did you pinch Elizabeth Hubbard this morning?
Tituba	Yes, the tall man brought her to me, and I pinched her.
Judge	Why did you go to Mr. Putnam's house last night and hurt her?
Tituba	They made me go. They pulled me there.
Judge	How did you get there?
Tituba	We rode on sticks and were there very quickly.
Judge	Do you ride through the trees, or do you ride over them?
Tituba	I don't know. We are just there so quickly.
Judge	Why did you not tell your master about this?
Tituba	I was afraid that they would cut off my head.
Judge	What did Sarah Osborne look like?
Tituba	She had a woman's head and two legs and wings.
	(Abigail Williams cried out that she saw this creature and that it turned into Sarah Osborne.)
Judge	What else have you seen?
Tituba	I saw a hairy thing, an ugly thing. It stands up like a man and has only two legs.
Judge	Did you see Sarah Good hurting Elizabeth Hubbard last Saturday?
Tituba	I did see her put a wolf on Elizabeth.
	(Elizabeth cries out that it is true: a wolf did attack her last Saturday.)
Judge	What does the man look like?
Tituba	He walks around in black clothes. I think he has white hair.
	(Ann cries out that she sees the man hovering above Sarah Good.)
Judge	What does the woman look like?
Tituba	She wears a hood made from black and white material.

Follow-Up Note: Tituba admitted that she was a witch. She remained in jail, but nothing more is said of her in town documents. We simply don't know what happened to her. We do know that she was not hanged.

Rebecca Nurse's Trial

Directions: Rebecca Nurse was a devout church member. Even so, it was a common belief at the time that witchcraft ran in families. Years before, Rebecca's mother was accused of being a witch. It never went to trial, but the people never forgot it. Rebecca was also known at times to argue with her neighbors. One argument took place over a group of pigs wandering into her yard. Nevertheless, Rebecca had an outstanding reputation. Her husband had been a financial success, too. The couple was a symbol of the prosperous Salem Town. When the split took place in Salem, he sided against the Salem Village. Ann Putnam's mother led the charge against Rebecca. While sick in her home, a minister visited Ann's mother. She was under some sort of attack that left her completely stiff. Then she began flailing her arms and legs and yelling for Rebecca Nurse to be gone. An argument took place between the invisible spirit of Rebecca and Ann's mother. The minister witnessed all of it—and Rebecca would answer for it in court.

The judge liked and respected Rebecca Nurse. He pleaded with her to confess so that they would not have to convict her. Rebecca stood her ground and insisted she was innocent of the charges.

Judge   (*talking to Ann Putnam*) Tell us if you have seen this woman hurt you.

Ann   Yes, she beat me this morning.

Judge   Abigail, did this woman hurt you?

Abigail   Yes.

        (*Ann's mother cries out that Rebecca has hurt her, too.*)

Judge   Goody Nurse, there are two people here, Ann Putnam and Abigail Williams, who say that you hurt them. How do you respond?

Rebecca   I can say that before God I am innocent. God will clear my name.

Judge   We all hope that you are innocent, but if you are guilty, God will discover it. Kenny, what do you have to say?

Kenny   When Rebecca came into my house, I was seized with sickness.

Judge   Here are not only these three witness, but also the wife of Mr. Putnam, Ann's mother. She said that you tempted her to turn away from God, and that you also hurt her.

Rebecca   I am innocent of this charge. I haven't left home in eight or nine days.

Rebecca Nurse's Trial *(cont.)*

Ann's Mother	Didn't you bring the black man with you? Didn't you tell me to tempt God and die? (*Faints and is so overcome that she must be carried from the courtroom.*)
Rebecca	Oh Lord, help me! (*She raises her hands, but when she does, three in the audience cry out as if she hurts them. Those around her cry out in pain every time she moves.*)
Mary Walcott	She hurt me, too. (*Elizabeth Hubbard says that she was hurt, also. Others in the crowd howl and cry out in pain.*)
Judge	What do you say to these two grown adults? They say you have hurt them.
Rebecca	God knows that I have not hurt them. I am innocent.
Judge	It is so awful to see all the suffering in these people, yet you stand there with dry eyes, unaffected by it all.
Rebecca	You do not know what is in my heart and how I feel.
Judge	You would do yourself a favor if you would only confess and give God the glory.
Rebecca	I am as innocent of these charges as an unborn baby would be.
Judge	You only need to confess and give glory to God. If you are innocent, I pray that God will clear you. But if you are guilty, I know he will discover it. Give me a straight answer: are you familiar with any of these spirits?
Rebecca	No. I am only familiar with the spirit of God alone.
Judge	What do you say to these charges that a black man whispered in your ear and yellow birds flying all about you? What do you say to these charges?
Rebecca	It is all false. I am clear of these charges.
Judge	Could it be possible that you are a witch but haven't been tempted yet?
Rebecca	No. (*People in the crowd fall into terrible fits and cry out.*)
Judge	Do you think these people are making this up? Are they making themselves suffer?
Rebecca	I cannot tell.
Judge	That is a strange answer. Everyone can judge for himself or herself.
Rebecca	I must be silent on this issue.

Rebecca Nurse's Trial *(cont.)*

Judge   They say you hurt them. If you think they are making this accusation up, then you must hate them and see them as murderers.

Rebecca   I cannot say what I think about it.

Judge   Well, then, say if you think they are really suffering.

Rebecca   I do not think they are pretending that they are suffering.

Judge   If you knew they were suffering, why did you never visit them at their homes?

Rebecca   I was afraid that I would fall into fits, too.

(People in the crowd fall into loud fits as Rebecca moves her arms.)

Judge   Do you believe these people are bewitched?

Rebecca   Yes, I do think so.

Judge   Why won't you admit that you are doing this to them?

Rebecca   Would you want me to lie?

Judge   Mrs. Putnam says that your spirit came to her and caused her fits. What do you think of this?

Rebecca   I cannot help if the Devil appears to people using my body.

(Rebecca holds her neck to one side, and Elizabeth Hubbard's neck follows her in the same position, as if being controlled by her. Abigail cries out that Rebecca will break her neck.)

Follow-Up Note: After a lengthy trial, the jury found Rebecca Nurse innocent on these charges. When this was announced, the courtroom erupted in anger. The judge and the accusers did not accept this decision. The jury became hesitant of its decision, and the judge asked the jurors to review the case one more time. The jury changed its verdict. Rebecca Nurse was hanged on July 19.

The Salem Witch Trials

A Statement from Ann

Directions: It has been 12 years since the trials in Salem. You, Ann Putnam, were a key player in those trials. Now you are an adult. You've had time to think about the trials and the many people who died professing their innocence. You know that you need to make peace with your neighbors. You consulted your minister, and he has offered to help you write this statement. How will you explain the outbursts? What do you have to say about your accusations? Write your statement and solve this mystery in the space below.

The Lincoln Assassination Conspiracy

Teacher Lesson Plan

Standard/Objective

❋ Demonstrate an understanding that different scholars may describe the same event or situation in different ways but must provide reasons for evidence for their views. (NCSS)

❋ Students will act out a simulated trial of eight people accused of conspiring to murder President Lincoln and then decide on the guilt or innocence of each suspect.

Materials

copies of *Attention Grabber* (page 48); copies of *Background Information* (pages 49–51); copies of *Graphic Organizer* (page 52); copies of *Suspects Charged in the Confederate Conspiracy* (pages 53–54); copies of *The Prosecution's Case* (pages 55–58); copies of *The Defense* (pages 59–60); copies of *A Letter in the Hotel* (page 61); copies of *Final Notes and the Verdict* (page 62)

Discussion Questions

❋ What kind of writing is this (for example, journal or diary writing)?

❋ What do you think this person is talking about?

❋ Why would someone write something like this?

❋ What is the most interesting phrase this person used?

❋ Describe the type of person who would write this in his or her journal.

The Activity: Day 1

Distribute copies of *Attention Grabber* (page 48) to students as they enter class. Give them a few minutes to read over it fully. Ask the discussion questions above. Some students might understand by the writing that it is about a murder. Have students read *Background Information* (pages 49–51). Then if students have not already guessed, tell them this is a diary entry written by John Wilkes Booth.

Explain to students that a terrible thing has just happened in our country: two weeks ago, the president was assassinated. It has been decided that the suspects will stand trial in a military court. Explain that they have been chosen to serve on a commission to decide the fate of the suspects. They were selected for this commission because of their high rank in the military. Some of them are even war heroes! Distribute copies of *Graphic Organizer* (page 52). This page will help remind students of the definitions of a military court, conspiracy, and murder.

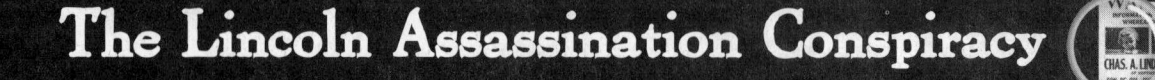
Teacher Lesson Plan *(cont.)*

The Activity: Day 1 *(cont.)*

Explain that military court is desirable in this situation for several reasons:

* ⁜ military trials are quicker
* ⁜ rules of evidence in a military court are not as strict, which can make the conviction much easier
* ⁜ the evidence can be applied to all the suspects because they can be tried as a group
* ⁜ convictions in military courts are rarely overturned

First, students must understand the difference between murder and conspiracy. The charge being brought against the suspects is conspiracy. Have students look up the word *conspiracy* in a dictionary. To be convicted of conspiracy, the defendants must be involved in the secret planning of the murder. The suspects are charged with conspiring with a group of Confederate officials to murder President Lincoln, Vice President Johnson, Secretary of State Seward, and General Grant. Explain that the trial will be presented in the same way it was presented back then. Then tell them the trial will begin tomorrow.

The Activity: Day 2

Distribute copies of the *Suspects Charged in the Confederate Conspiracy* (pages 53–54) to each student. These two pages will give the commission information on each suspect. Give students enough time to read the information and ask any questions.

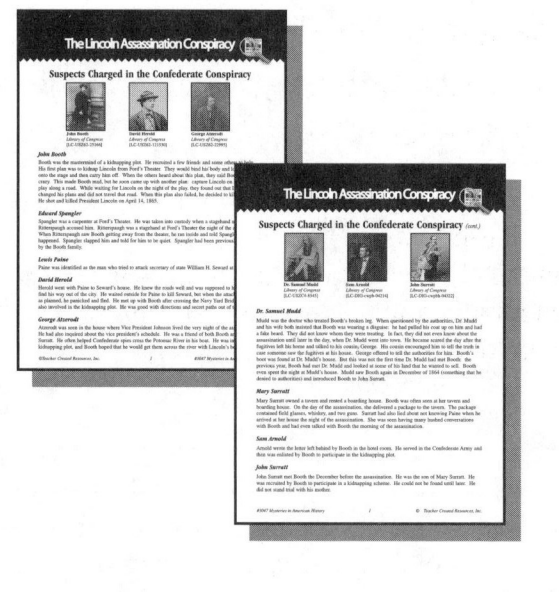

Begin by having students define "prosecution" and "defense" lawyers. They must understand the difference before having the trial.

First, the commission will hear the prosecution's case. Assign a student to each statement. Have them act as witnesses and read the information to the class. When all lines have been read, distribute copies of *The Prosecution's Case* (pages 55–58). This is a copy of the testimony for the students. They are allowed to take notes on these pages but must not talk about the evidence amongst themselves. When the letter from Samuel Arnold is mentioned, distribute *A Letter in the Hotel* (page 61) for everyone to read. Make sure that students keep the prosecution notes handy for the following days.

Teacher Lesson Plan *(cont.)*

The Activity: Day 3

On this day the commission gets to hear the defense side of the story. Have students take out *The Prosecution's Case* from the previous day. Read over it to have the information fresh in everyone's mind. Then assign a student to read each defense statement. When all have been read, distribute copies of *The Defense* (pages 59–60). This is just a copy of what they have heard. Remind students that they can take notes on this page and that they are still not allowed to talk about the case with each other. Explain that they will have the opportunity to deliberate the verdicts the following day.

The Activity: Day 4

This is the day for the commission to deliberate the verdicts of the eight defendants. Have students take out *The Prosecution's Case* and *The Defense*. Read over these one more time, comparing what the prosecution said and what the defense said. Let students talk openly about their opinions on this case. Encourage students to take notes during the deliberation. When everyone has had the opportunity to speak his or her thoughts, take a vote on each defendant: guilty or not guilty of conspiracy to commit murder. Then have students come up with their punishment. Remind students that back then criminals were hanged if given the death penalty. In addition, remind students that the death penalty could only be given if the prosecution had proved its case on all points.

The Activity: Day 5

Distribute copies of *Final Notes and the Verdict* (page 62) as students arrive for class. Read it together as a class. Then make a Venn diagram on the board and have students compare the similarities and differences of both verdicts. Let students discuss this further. If time permits, allow students to go on the Internet and read other theories about the Lincoln assassination. They might also want to find out more about spies in the Civil War or what finally happened to Jefferson Davis.

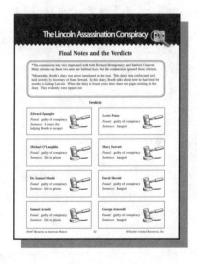

Attention Grabber

April 14

I struck boldly, and not as the papers say. I walked with a firm step through a thousand of his friends... A colonel was at his side.

In jumping, broke my leg. I passed all his pickets. Rode sixty miles last night, with the bone of my left tearing the flesh at every jump.

I can never repent it though we hated to kill. Our country owed all our troubles to him, and God simply made me the instrument of his punishment.

Background Information

Strangely, not long before he was assassinated, President Lincoln had a dream. He dreamed that a corpse was lying in a coffin in the East Wing of the White House. He followed the crowd of people into the room to pay his respects. When he inquired who was dead, he was told it was the president.

All history books agree that John Wilkes Booth shot and killed President Abraham Lincoln. What is a mystery, however, is the idea of a conspiracy ring surrounding Lincoln's assassination. Eight people were tried for conspiracy to commit this murder. Were they guilty? Who was really involved in the planning of this murder? Did Jefferson Davis, the Confederate president, plan it? Were people in Lincoln's own government a part of the conspiracy? Some theories point to this.

John Booth

The night of the assassination, Booth arrived at Ford's Theater. He knew the theater well because he performed there often. It was no shock to anyone to see his face. Booth entered backstage. He had someone hold his horse's reins right outside the door. He gave the excuse that his horse would try to escape if he tried to tie him to a hitching post. Soldiers were outside the front of the theater keeping guard. One police officer named John Parker was on duty just outside the presidential box. At about 10 P.M., Booth went through the hall that led to the presidential box. For some unknown reason, Parker was not there. The president had no guard to protect him. He made his way into the box where the president was sitting and fired his gun. After shooting President Lincoln, Booth jumped down onto the stage and yelled, "*Sic semper tyrannis,*" meaning "Thus ever to tyrants!" As he jumped, Booth's spur became caught in the flag that draped the box. He lost his balance and fractured his leg in the fall.

more to follow

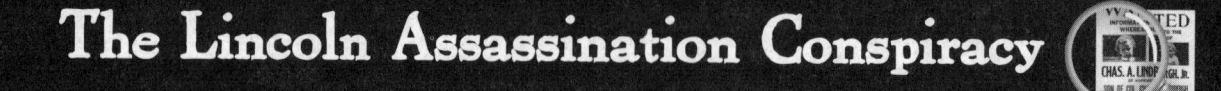

Background Information *(cont.)*

That very evening (at precisely the same time), Lewis Paine had tried to assassinate the secretary of state, William H. Seward. Paine disguised himself as a messenger bringing medicine to Seward, who had been hurt in a carriage accident. He entered Seward's home and beat Seward's son with a pistol. Then he made his way into the bedroom where two family members and a nurse valiantly fought him off. While he fled the house, he stabbed and killed a state department messenger at the door. David Herold, a friend of Paine's, had gone with Paine to Seward's house. Herold waited outside for Paine to kill Seward, but when the attack did not go as planned, he panicked and fled.

Were these two crimes just a coincidence? Were there more crimes planned for that very evening? Or should this one night have resulted in four murders? Was that Booth's original plan?

George Atzerodt was a friend of John Surratt and lived with the Surratt family for a while. Atzerodt had stayed at the Surratt boarding house in March, when both Paine and Booth were seen there. He spent his nights ferrying Confederate spies across the Potomac River. The night of the assassination, Atzerodt had been seen in the house where Vice President Andrew Johnson lived. It was wondered if he was supposed to kill the vice president that night.

Michael O'Laughlin went to elementary school with Booth. They were close friends and even lived next door to each other for a while. On April 13, O'Laughlin was seen in front of the secretary of war's home. General Grant was visiting the home at the time and came out to greet the people. O'Laughlin demanded to see the general. He put up such a fuss that the sergeant accompanying Grant ordered O'Laughlin to leave the area. O'Laughlin was seen visiting Booth that very day. Was O'Laughlin scouting his prey, General Grant? After all, Grant was supposed to attend the play with the Lincolns the night of the assassination.

more to follow

Background Information *(cont.)*

Guards were in their places around the capital city that night. Immediately after Lincoln was shot, telegrams were sent to the guards. These telegrams told the guards that the president had been shot and to be on the lookout for the killer. Booth made his way to the Navy Yard Bridge, where Sergeant Silas T. Cobb was on duty. Cobb had not received the telegram yet, so he had no reason to suspect anyone. Booth told the officer his name and that he had been in town late on business. He just wanted to get home right across the bridge. Cobb let him through.

A man named John Fletcher owned a stable business. Fletcher had loaned a horse to David Herold, Paine's friend, the day Lincoln was assassinated. He saw Herold fleeing toward the outskirts of town and followed in hot pursuit, hoping to get his horse back. He complained to police, but the police were too busy with the assassination to worry about a stolen horse. Herold met up with Booth after crossing the Navy Yard Bridge.

Booth and Herold went to a tavern owned by the Surratt family. They took a field glass, rifle, and whiskey from the tavern. Booth was in tremendous pain by this point, so they tried to find a doctor. Booth and Herold went to see Dr. Samuel Mudd at his home. They arrived in the middle of the night and told the doctor that Booth had fallen from his horse. Dr. Mudd agreed to see the patient and treated his leg. Later that day, both Booth and Herold left. Twelve days after the assassination, they finally ended up on a farm owned by a man named Garrett. It was there that detectives caught up with the two men. They were inside the barn. Herold came out and was arrested. Booth refused to come out, so they set the barn on fire in hopes of forcing Booth out. Other accounts believe Booth committed suicide there. There's even one small town in Texas that claims Booth escaped and lived there under an assumed name! The police report said that one of the detectives aimed at Booth and shot. His body was dragged from the barn and taken to the front porch, where he died within hours.

Graphic Organizer

Reasons for a Military Court

_____
_____
_____
_____

What is the difference between conspiracy and murder?

_____
_____
_____
_____
_____
_____

Define *prosecution.*

_____
_____
_____
_____
_____

Define *defense.*

_____
_____
_____
_____
_____

The Lincoln Assassination Conspiracy

Suspects Charged in the Confederate Conspiracy

John Booth
Library of Congress
[LC-USZ62-25166]

David Herold
Library of Congress
[LC-USZ62-121530]

George Atzerodt
Library of Congress
[LC-USZ62-22995]

John Booth

Booth was the mastermind of a kidnapping plot. He recruited a few friends and some others to help. His first plan was to kidnap Lincoln from Ford's Theater. They would bind his body and lower him onto the stage and then carry him off. When the others heard about this plan, they said Booth was crazy. This made Booth mad, but he soon came up with another plan: capture Lincoln on his way to a play along a road. While waiting for Lincoln on the night of the play, they found out that Lincoln changed his plans and did not travel that road. When this plan also failed, he decided to kill Lincoln. He shot and killed President Lincoln on April 14, 1865.

Edward Spangler

Spangler was a carpenter at Ford's Theater. He was taken into custody when a stagehand named Jacob Ritterspaugh accused him. Ritterspaugh was a stagehand at Ford's Theater the night of the assassination. When Ritterspaugh saw Booth getting away from the theater, he ran inside and told Spangler what had happened. Spangler slapped him and told him to be quiet. Spangler had been previously employed by the Booth family.

Lewis Paine

Paine was identified as the man who tried to attack secretary of state William H. Seward at his house.

David Herold

Herold went with Paine to Seward's house. He knew the roads well and was supposed to help Paine find his way out of the city. He waited outside for Paine to kill Seward, but when the attack did not go as planned, he panicked and fled. He met up with Booth after crossing the Navy Yard Bridge. He was also involved in the kidnapping plot. He was good with directions and secret paths out of the area.

George Atzerodt

Atzerodt was seen in the house where Vice President Johnson lived the very night of the assassination. He had also inquired about the vice president's schedule. He was a friend of both Booth and John Surratt. He often helped Confederate spies cross the Potomac River in his boat. He was involved in the kidnapping plot, and Booth hoped that he would get them across the river with Lincoln's body.

Suspects Charged in the Confederate Conspiracy *(cont.)*

Dr. Samual Mudd
Library of Congress
[LC-USZC4-8545]

Sam Arnold
Library of Congress
[LC-DIG-cwpb-04214]

John Surratt
Library of Congress
[LC-DIG-cwpbh-04322]

Dr. Samuel Mudd

Mudd was the doctor who treated Booth's broken leg. When questioned by the authorities, Dr. Mudd and his wife both insisted that Booth was wearing a disguise: he had pulled his coat up on him and had a fake beard. They did not know whom they were treating. In fact, they did not even know about the assassination until later in the day, when Dr. Mudd went into town. He became scared the day after the fugitives left his home and talked to his cousin, George. His cousin encouraged him to tell the truth in case someone saw the fugitives at his house. George offered to tell the authorities for him. Booth's boot was found at Dr. Mudd's house. But this was not the first time Dr. Mudd had met Booth: the previous year, Booth had met Dr. Mudd and looked at some of his land that he wanted to sell. Booth even spent the night at Mudd's house. Mudd saw Booth again in December of 1864 (something that he denied to authorities) and introduced Booth to John Surratt.

Mary Surratt

Mary Surratt owned a tavern and rented a boarding house. Booth was often seen at her tavern and boarding house. On the day of the assassination, she delivered a package to the tavern. The package contained field glasses, whiskey, and two guns. Surratt had also lied about not knowing Paine when he arrived at her house the night of the assassination. She was seen having many hushed conversations with Booth and had even talked with Booth the morning of the assassination.

Sam Arnold

Arnold wrote the letter left behind by Booth in the hotel room. He served in the Confederate Army and then was enlisted by Booth to participate in the kidnapping plot.

John Surratt

John Surratt met Booth the December before the assassination. He was the son of Mary Surratt. He was recruited by Booth to participate in a kidnapping scheme. He could not be found until later. He did not stand trial with his mother.

The Lincoln Assassination Conspiracy

The Prosecution's Case

The prosecution is the side that accuses. They try to prove the case against the defendant. First the prosecution needs to prove there was a Confederate plot. Here are two witnesses who took the stand.

Richard Montgomery, Union Spy

"I live in Canada, and I was a spy for the Union Army. There were several members of the Canadian cabinet who told me that the South had many assassins planted all over the North. They were ready to kill Lincoln, Stanton, and Grant, as well as a few others when the word was given to do so. I can tell you right now that one of these cabinet members talked to John Wilkes Booth himself! Booth had gone to Montreal at least three times to talk about this plot in detail."

Sanford Conover, former member of the Confederate War Department in Richmond, VA

"I left Richmond in 1863 and moved to Canada. I knew every member of the Richmond cabinets and the Canadian cabinets. I was especially close to the Confederate Jacob Thompson, who you may have recalled was on Vice President Johnson's most-wanted list. Jacob Thompson told me about Booth's plan. In fact, I was in Thompson's office the day John Surratt paid him a visit. He came bringing messages about the assassination from Jefferson Davis. I waited until Thompson finished reading the letters. He looked up and said, 'This makes the thing all right.'"

The Prosecution's Case *(cont.)*

Second, the prosecution has to prove that the suspects had planned to commit murder (and not kidnapping) from the very beginning.

Prosecutor Bingham

"Many have talked about this kidnapping scheme. We all know about it. But let me assure you that the suspects did not intend on kidnapping, they planned to murder. Let me describe this kidnapping plot for you, and you will see how it is absolutely ridiculous. Remember the part where Booth planned on hog-tying Lincoln up and lowering him down on to the stage? Even Booth would not come up with such a ridiculous plan!"

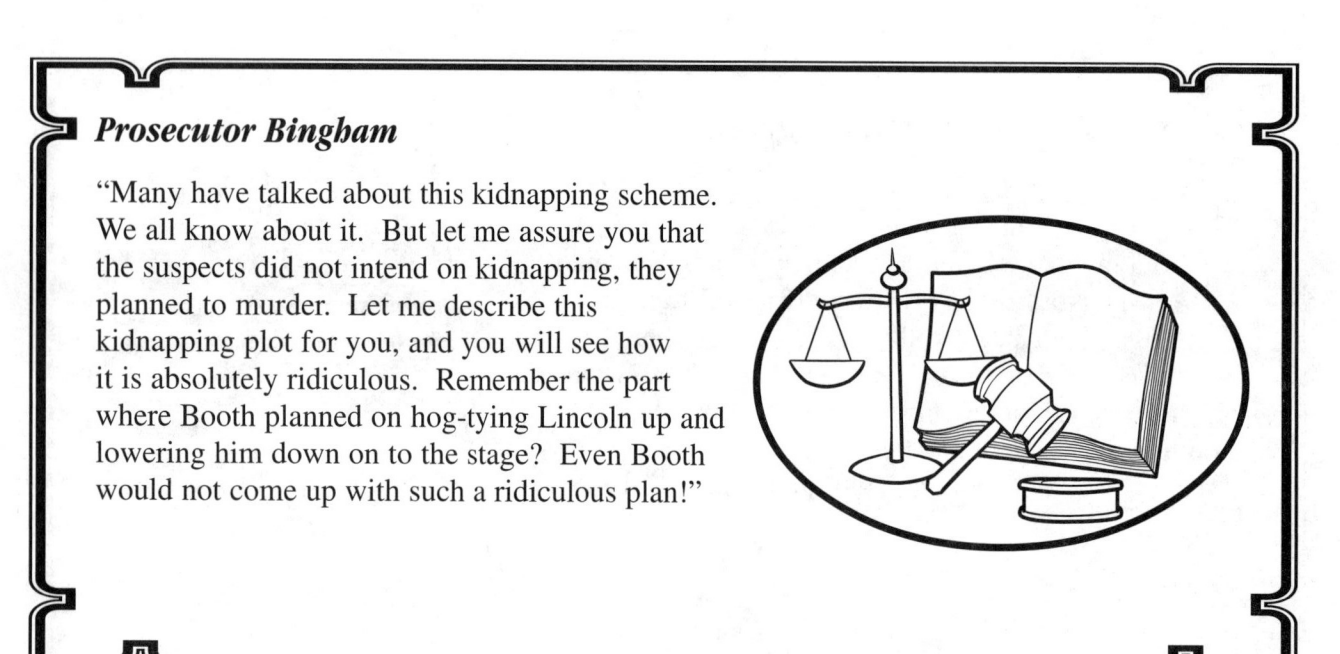

Policeman at Lincoln's 2nd Inauguration

"While I was patrolling the crowd at Lincoln's 2nd inauguration, there was a man who looked like Booth. The reason I remember him is that he tried to break through our line of protection during the ceremony. It made quite a scene. My friend, also a policeman, can testify to the same incident."

The Prosecution's Case *(cont.)*

Finally, the prosecution could focus on trying the suspects. All suspects were tried together, and there was no order to the testimony. The following information and quotes were given as testimony against the suspects.

David Herold

"I saw David Herold near Seward's house on April 14th."

"David Herold was with Booth when they were cornered in the barn on Garrett's farm."

Lewis Paine

"Lewis Paine was the man in Seward's house who attacked him. I saw him clear as a bell."

George Atzerodt

"I overheard Atzerodt asking about Vice President Johnson's daily schedule."

"If he did not want to commit murder, then why didn't he tell authorities? He had plenty of time to notify the people in charge of this plot to kill."

Samuel Arnold & Michael O'Laughlin

"Just look at the letter written by Samuel Arnold to Booth. Even Michael's name was there. They had to be a part of this murder plot."

Edward Spangler

"He told me not to tell which way Booth had gone the night of the assassination."

"He held the door open for Booth to escape. He held the door firmly shut to those who tried to follow Booth so that Booth could get away."

The Prosecution's Case *(cont.)*

Dr. Samuel Mudd

"Dr. Mudd is a Southerner at heart. He allowed Confederate couriers to hide on his property."

"Dr. Mudd was good friends with Mary Surratt's husband when he was alive. Everyone knows that Mr. Surratt allowed Confederate spies to stay at his house."

"I was there the night Mudd introduced Booth to John Surratt on December 23 in Washington. I saw Booth and Mudd having hushed conversations. It even looked like they were drawing a map on an envelope."

Mary Surratt

"I was a boarder in her house and saw Mary having a hushed conversation with Booth the morning of the assassination. In fact, I remember them having many hushed conversations."

"Mary rode with me to the tavern the morning of the assassination. She delivered a package for Booth. It was to have two guns, whiskey, and a field glass. Booth would be picking this up that very night."

"Mary lied when she denied she knew Lewis Paine. He showed up at her house when detectives were interrogating her. She said she had never seen him before."

The Lincoln Assassination Conspiracy

The Defense

The defense is the side that tries to prove that the accusations against them are false. They try to prove that they are innocent of the charge.

David Herold

"David Herold is a weak person. Really, he is very childlike. He is so easily led astray."

Lewis Paine

"My client is insane. When he tried to attack Seward at his house, Paine yelled out, 'I'm mad! I'm mad!' Just look at his behavior in court today. He is not normal. He hasn't paid any attention to any of the testimony. He walks in here with his head held high. He does not understand what is happening, and he did not know what he was doing when he attacked Seward."

Additional Information: In response to the insanity claim, the prosecutors called in their doctors to examine Paine. These doctors said he knew what he had done.

Michael O'Laughlin

"Michael was with us, his friends, the night of the murder. We can prove he was with us!"

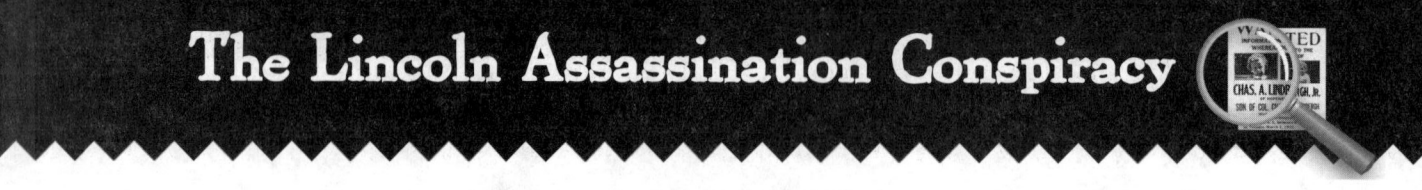
The Defense *(cont.)*

Dr. Samuel Mudd

"He's not sure why he lied about seeing Booth in Washington on December 23."

"He is a law-abiding citizen. Never done anyone any harm. He was only doing his job when he took care of Booth's leg."

George Atzerodt

George Atzerodt wrote this letter in his own defense and his lawyer read it for him. None of the suspects were allowed to testify.

"On the evening of the 14th of April, I met Booth and Paine at the Herndon House, in this city at eight o'clock. He (Booth) said he himself would murder Mr. Lincoln and General Grant, Paine should take Mr. Seward, and I should take Mr. Johnson. I told him I would not do it; that I had gone into the thing to capture, but I was not going to kill. He told me I was a fool…that it was death for every man who backed out; and so we parted. I wandered about the streets until about two o'clock in the morning, and (eventually) went to my cousin's house in Montgomery County, where I was arrested."

Mary Surratt

"Mary is an upstanding citizen. She attends mass regularly and would never think of murdering anyone, especially the president!"

"Mary did not recognize Lewis Paine because she has poor eyesight. The other borders did not recognize him at first because he was messy and wearing a hat."

"Mary only delivered a package for Booth because she was a kind lady and wanted to help anyone who needed her. She was going to the tavern anyway on a business matter."

A Letter in the Hotel

This letter was found in John Booth's hotel room after the assassination. It has three names in it: John, Sam, and Mike.

March 27, 1865

Dear John:

Was business so important that you could not remain in Balto. til I saw you? I came in as soon as I could, but found you had gone to W——n. I called also to see Mike... You know full well that the G——t suspects something is going on there; therefore the undertaking is becoming more complicated. Why not, for the present, desist?... Do not act rashly or in haste. I would refer your first query, "Go and see how it will be taken at R——d."

Write me in Balto., as I expect to be in about Wednesday or Thursday, or, if you can possibly come on, I will Tuesday meet you in Balto., at B——. Ever I subscribe myself.

Your friend,

Sam

Final Notes and the Verdicts

*The commission was very impressed with both Richard Montgomery and Sanford Conover. Many citizens say these two men are habitual liars, but the commission ignored those citizens.

*Meanwhile, Booth's diary was never mentioned in the trial. This diary was confiscated and held secretly by Secretary of State Seward. In this diary, Booth talks about how he had tried for months to kidnap Lincoln. When the diary is found years later, there are pages missing in the diary. They evidently were ripped out.

Verdicts

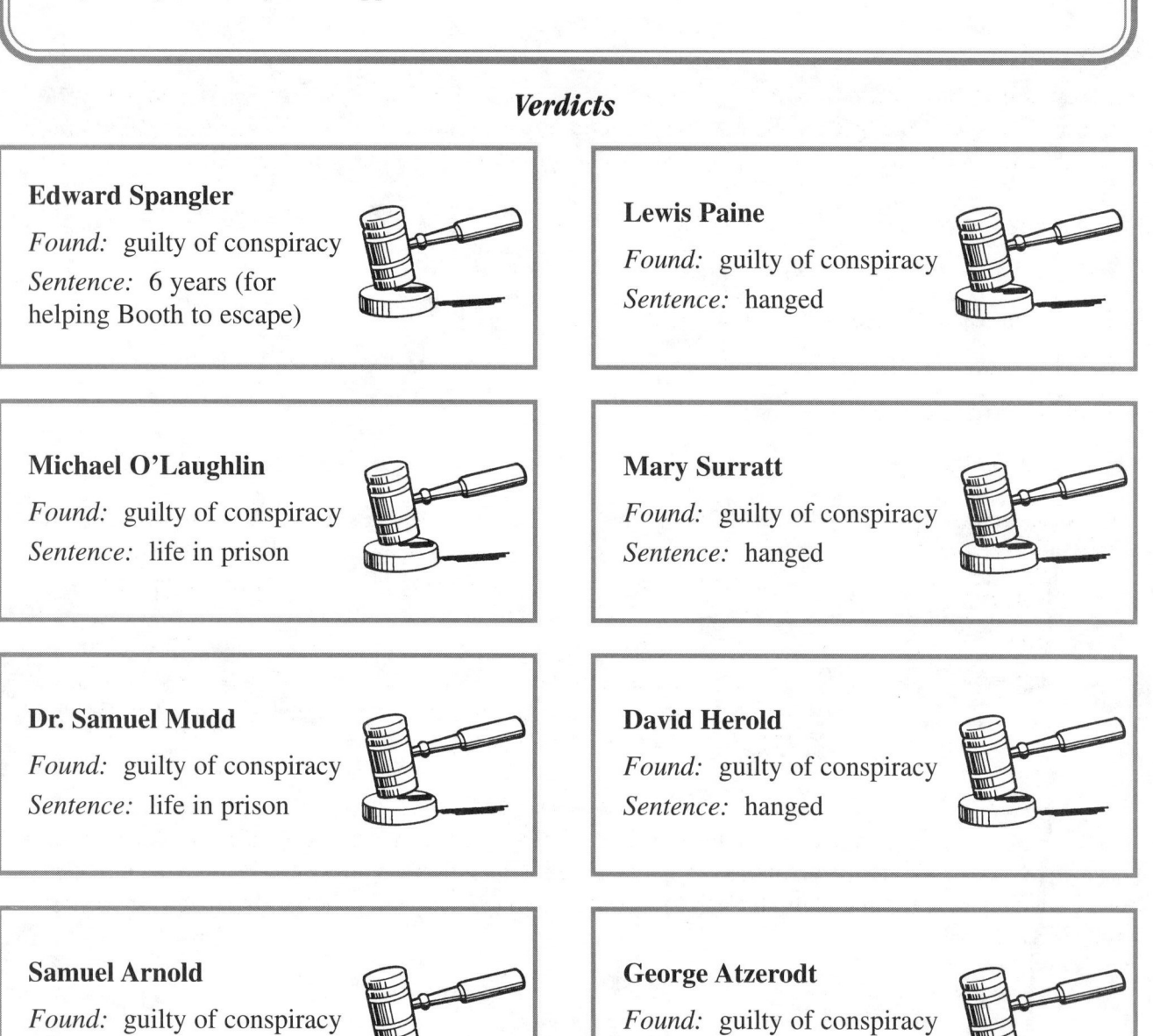

Edward Spangler

Found: guilty of conspiracy

Sentence: 6 years (for helping Booth to escape)

Lewis Paine

Found: guilty of conspiracy

Sentence: hanged

Michael O'Laughlin

Found: guilty of conspiracy

Sentence: life in prison

Mary Surratt

Found: guilty of conspiracy

Sentence: hanged

Dr. Samuel Mudd

Found: guilty of conspiracy

Sentence: life in prison

David Herold

Found: guilty of conspiracy

Sentence: hanged

Samuel Arnold

Found: guilty of conspiracy

Sentence: life in prison

George Atzerodt

Found: guilty of conspiracy

Sentence: hanged

The Explosion on the Maine

Teacher Lesson Plan

Standard/Objective

✳ Locate, access, analyze, organize, and apply information about selected public issues, recognizing and explaining multiple points of view. (NCSS)

✳ Students will write and perform a play about the explosion on the *U.S.S. Maine* and then write a letter to a man who survived the explosion explaining their decision concerning who was responsible.

Materials

copies of *Attention Grabber* (page 66); copies of *George Preston Blow Letter* (page 67); copies of *Graphic Organizer* (page 68); copies of *Background Information* (pages 69–71); copies of *The Plan for the U.S.S. Maine Play* (page 72); copies of *A Letter to George Preston Blow* (page 73)

Discussion Questions

✳ What is the *Maine*?

✳ What do you think the newspaper article is about?

✳ What is the Spanish cruiser *Alfonso XII*?

✳ In what ways could this event be a mystery?

The Activity: Day 1

Just before students enter the classroom, hang a sign over the classroom door that says, "You are now entering February 15, 1898." When students sit down, ask them if they know what is going on in the world. Most students probably will not know, but others might say the Spanish American War. Tell students that you have a copy of an article from the *New York Times* from the year 1898. Distribute *Attention Grabber* (page 66). This is a reproduction of part of an article that was printed the day following the explosion of the *Maine*. Have students read it silently.

Have students form groups with 4 or 5 students to a group. Then ask the discussion questions above. Give each group enough time to talk about these questions. After each group has had plenty of time to talk about the questions, tell students that this article was about a ship that exploded off the coast of Cuba and brought the United States into a war with Spain.

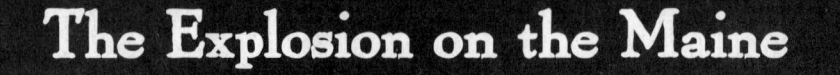

Teacher Lesson Plan *(cont.)*

The Activity: Day 1 (cont.)

Distribute the *George Preston Blow Letter* (page 67). Explain to students that this man was on the ship when it exploded. He survived and wrote this letter to his wife the following day. Read this aloud to the class.

Finally, distribute copies of *Background Information* (pages 69–71) to the class. Have students form their groups again. Let students in each group take turns reading these pages aloud. Then distribute *Graphic Organizer* (page 68). On this graphic-organizer ship, students will be drawing all the different possibilities of how the *Maine* exploded. They will also make a legend to explain their symbols.

The Activity: Day 2

Write this question on the board: "What caused the explosion on the *Maine*?" Let students look back at their graphic organizers and the background information. Try to get students talking about this mystery explosion.

Have students list all the possibilities on the board. There should be at least three different ideas: the Spanish are responsible, the Cuban rebels are responsible, or the *Maine* malfunctioned. (Other students might want to add that Americans who want the war are responsible.) Tell students that they will be working in groups to write a play that reenacts this event. Students should be placed into groups according to their theories of the mystery. (For example, those who think the Spanish are responsible should be grouped together with others who agree with that theory. For time sake, there should not be more than five groups.) Note: If there are students who cannot decide on a theory to believe, then you might want to assign students to a group. Explain that it doesn't matter if students agree with their theory or not; they are just to show how this could be a viable theory through their reenactment.

Distribute the student activity sheet *The Plan for the U.S.S. Maine Play* (page 72). Let students work on ideas for their plays in their groups. Let students spend the remaining time organizing the ideas for their plays.

The Activity: Day 3

Tell students that they will begin writing their plays today. Have them use information on their graphic organizers, background information, and student activity sheets to help them write. Instruct students that their plays should be between 4 and 8 minutes long. If groups finish writing, they can practice performing the plays. Tell students that it is okay to use scripts if they need to during the performance the following day. Also, some students might want to bring in props or costumes for their play.

Teacher Lesson Plan *(cont.)*

The Activity: Day 4

Let each group finish writing their play. You might want to make copies for the group so that every person has a copy in their hand. Then give groups time to practice their plays. Finally, let each group perform their play for the class.

Ask the following questions: "Who had the most convincing theory? What made it convincing?" Let students spend some time discussing their answers.

The Activity: Day 5

Finally, distribute the student activity sheet *A Letter to George Preston Blow* (page 73). Each student will be writing a letter to George Preston Blow, the man who survived the explosion in 1898. This letter will include an opinion about the explosion on the *Maine* and reasons for this theory. This activity not only makes students use higher-level thinking skills as they make judgments and try to convince George Preston Blow of their theory, they are also using their creativity. If time permits, let students share their letters in small groups. Make sure you collect these letters for assessment.

> As an added extension, let students view the website *www.spanamwar.com* to learn more about the Spanish American War.

Attention Grabber

The New York Times

FEBRUARY 16, 1898

THE MAINE BLOWN UP!

Terrible Explosion on Board the United States Battleship in Havana Harbor

MANY PERSONS KILLED AND WOUNDED

**All the Boats of the Spanish
Cruiser *Alfonso XII* Assisting
in the Work of Relief**

Havana, Feb. 15 - At 9:45 o'clock this evening a terrible explosion took place on board the United States battleship *Maine* in Havana Harbor.

As yet the cause of the explosion is not apparent. The wounded sailors of the Maine are unable to explain it. It is believed that the battleship is totally destroyed.

WHAT SENOR DE LOME SAYS

He Declares That No Spaniard Would Be Guilty of Causing Such a Disaster

Senor de Lome, the departing ex-Minister of Spain to this country, who arrived in this city last night, and went to the Hotel St. Marc, at Fifth Avenue and Thirty-ninth Street, was awakened on the receipt of the news from Havana.

He refused to believe the report at first. When he had been assured of the truth of the story he said that there was no possibility that the Spaniards had anything to do with the destruction of the Maine.

No Spaniard, he said, would be guilty of such an act. If the report was true, he said, the explosion must have been caused by some accident on board the warship.

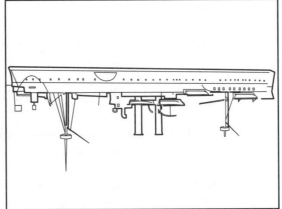

**None of the Wounded Men Able
to Give Any Explanation of the
Cause of the Disaster**

The explosion shook the whole city. The windows were broken in nearly all the houses.

The correspondent of the Associated Press says he has conversed with several of the wounded sailors and understands from them that the explosion took place while they were asleep, so that they can give no particulars as to the cause.

Many persons were killed or wounded. All the boats of the Spanish cruiser *Alfonso XII* are assisting.

George Preston Blow Letter

February 16, 1898

On Board: S.S. City of Washington

Dearest,

I sent you two cablegrams last night telling you of my safety, and hoping they both reached you before the morning papers, and that you were spared the agony of suspense and uncertainty.

It seems almost selfish to speak of ourselves even when so many hundreds are mourning lost dear ones. Still I could only give you the brief statement that I was safe and unhurt.

I can not tell you now of my miraculous escape, as the scene is still too terrible to recall, even had I the time. I will only say that I was in my room, writing to you when the ship blew up, and that when I rushed for the ladder leading on deck I found the door closed. In pitch darkness, with explosion following explosion, and expecting each second to be blown into the air, or drowned by the inrushing water, I found the other door and reached the ladder—probably the last.

The whole ship was blown into the air, except the officer's quarters—which explains why so many of them were saved. In fact we only lost two, and only a few were slightly wounded. Among the men, we saved about 50, leaving about 250 dead. I can not write of the horrors now. Each man lived a lifetime of horror in a few seconds and all would like to forget it if possible.

Whether we were torpedoed by the Spanish, blown up by a mine, or whether the Cubans did it to bring on a war—or whether it was one of these spontaneous explosions, we do not know. I hate to suspect the Spanish, and their actions; sympathy and assistance seems to indicate that they are ignorant of the cause. For the present we must withhold our judgment.

It is almost certain that Congress will declare war today, without waiting—and it is possible that we may be prisoners before night. If so you must not worry, as we are sure to receive good treatment on account of the sympathy of the people.

I escaped in my trousers, undershirt and socks. Of course I lost my glasses and haven't a cent in the world. The Captain will look out for us when he gets time. At present we have other and sadder duties to our lost shipmates.

Do not worry about me darling, for I am strong and able to stand whatever may come—be it what it may. If we were destroyed by treachery, we must avenge our dead when the opportunity occurs.

In my struggle in the darkness and water, you and the babies were in my mind, dearest. I found time to help one poor devil to climb to a place of safety. Whether he escaped or who he was I do not know. Nearly all the saved among the crew were people who had blown overboard and afterwards picked up. One man was picked up a hundred yards away.

The mail steamer has arrived and brought me your two dear letters of the 9th and 10th. As the mail goes out again immediately I must stop and read them and see if they require immediate answer.

Well, dearest, I have read the letters and find they contain good news so I will not attempt to answer them now.

God bless you dearest. He has been very good to us.

Love and kisses for the dear little ones and a heart full to bursting of love and longing for you my darling.

I must go to work, love to all, Preston

Graphic Organizer

Directions: Using the ship below, draw symbols at the appropriate place on the ship to show the different theories about the explosion on the *Maine*. (For example, draw a symbol for the mine by drawing it in the water around the ship.) After drawing the symbols, make a legend that explains the meaning of the symbols. Show at least four theories using these symbols.

Legend

Symbol	Meaning

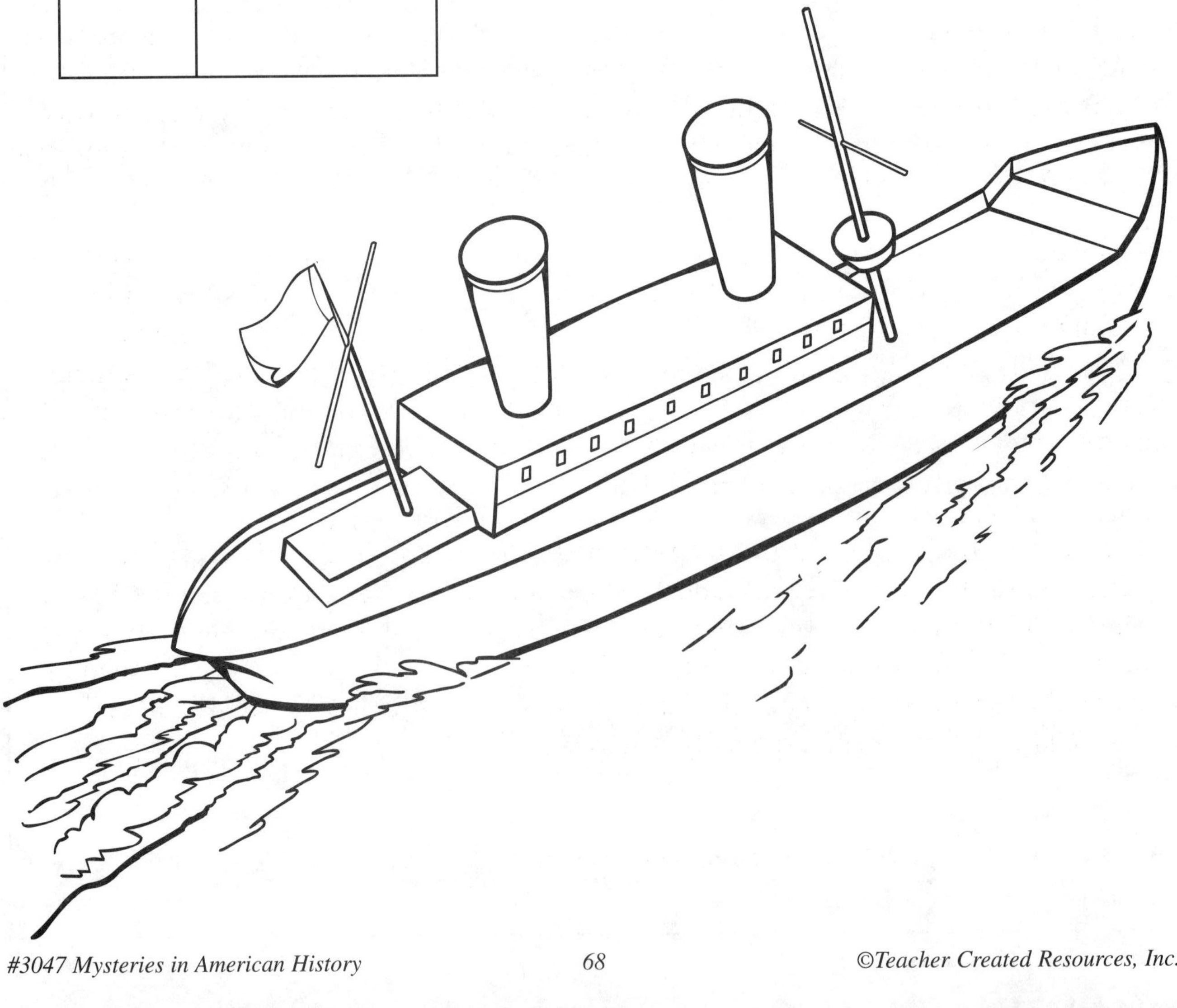

The Explosion on the Maine

Background Information

The *U.S.S. Maine* was one of the first modern battleships built by the United States. It was longer than a football field and took almost nine years to build. It was sent on a peace mission to Havana, Cuba, in January 1898.

At that time, Cuba was a colony of Spain. Years before, in 1868, the native Cubans revolted against the harsh treatments inflicted upon them by the Spanish. This rebellion began a war that lasted for many years. Some Americans supported the revolution and viewed the natives as freedom fighters. In 1873, a ship sailed from New York with a cargo of ammunition for the rebels. The Spanish hastily shot 53 crew members, including many Americans. In 1878, the Spanish promised to reform its government in Cuba, but this reform did not last long, and the Spaniards returned to their harsh executions and unwarranted arrests among the Cuban natives.

In 1895, another revolution swept across Cuba. Since the rebels were outnumbered five to one, they began guerrilla warfare. Because there was little money for guns, the Cubans used machetes when fighting the Spanish. But their most deadly weapon was the yellow fever. The natives had a high resistance against the infection, but the Spanish troops suffered more deaths from the fever than from anything else.

The Cubans sent propaganda disguised as news stories to reputable American papers. They also sent these stories to the "yellow press." The yellow press was known for attracting readers by printing sensational stories. These stories ignited emotion in people. William Hearst bought the *New York Journal* and began running sensational stories, including stories against Spain. The public was persuaded by these stories. They began to voice their disapproval of how the current U.S. president, William McKinley, was ignoring the problem in Cuba.

In September of 1897, President McKinley began to put pressure on the Spanish government to stop the violence against the Cubans or face war with the United States. Spain complied, even allowing some Cubans a say in their government until the rebels demanded full independence. Fearing the Spanish government had let up too much, in January of 1898 many Spaniards in Cuba began protesting in the streets, and angry crowds attacked foreigners, especially Americans.

more to follow

Background Information *(cont.)*

In hopes of deterring Spanish violence, McKinley ordered the *U.S.S. Maine* to Havana. After the *Maine* arrived on January 15, 1898, things seemed to quiet down until the Spanish ambassador to the United States wrote an insulting letter about McKinley that found its way into the yellow press. This letter called McKinley a "low politician." Americans screamed for blood, but the ambassador resigned before any violence occurred.

Sailors aboard the *Maine* were given shore leave, and many spent time buying local goods. While attending a local bullfight, Captain Sigsbee received a nasty note from some Spaniards threatening the *Maine*. The ship was put on high alert.

At 9:30 P.M. on February 15, the *Maine* exploded and sank. Most of the officers were unhurt because they were already in their quarters for the night. The ship's captain, Captain Sigsbee, escaped, as well. Men were blown into the air, and one man was found more than 100 feet away. About 266 men died in this explosion.

The officers had many differing ideas of who was to blame for this explosion. George Preston Blow, a lieutenant aboard the ship when it exploded, survived and wrote his questions about the explosion in his letter to his wife the following day. He wondered if the Spanish torpedoed the ship. He thought a mine floating in the water could have caused it, too. The Cubans were also mentioned, as he thought they could have done it to bring on a war to free themselves from the Spanish.

The naval board of inquiry conducted a study of the wreckage, and they concluded that the explosion came from a mine in the water. The Spanish sent its own board of inquiry and concluded that the explosion came from within the ship, possibly a boiler.

Even though investigations did not prove who did it beyond a reasonable doubt, the yellow press printed stories claiming the Spanish planted a mine and caused the explosion. In fact, a popular story says that the owner of the *New York Journal* told his reporter in Cuba just to worry about getting good pictures and that he would make the war happen. These newspapers said that it was the Spanish who set off a mine in the water to destroy the ship. The American people went wild and demanded a war. This eventually pressured the president, who would have liked to resolve this conflict peacefully, into war. The American public cried for revenge, and on April 25, 1898, Congress declared war on Spain.

more to follow

Background Information *(cont.)*

Ever since this event, mystery has surrounded this explosion. Was this explosion an accident, or was it a calculated event? If it was planned, who had the motive for war? The Spanish were definitely insulted that the U.S. would send a ship to their territory. What right did the U.S. have to stick their nose into another country's business? What did the Spanish have to gain if a war began with the U.S.? They certainly were not as strong militarily as the U.S. If it was a mine, did it break loose from the harbor defense and accidentally float towards the ship? Or did the Spanish plant it on purpose? A mine would have exploded under water. This explosion would have caused a geyser, and a shock wave would have been felt on the land. No one witnessed either of these—but it was dark outside.

The Cuban rebels were definitely interested in starting a war. They wanted the U.S. to give them freedom from the Spanish. They had sent inflated stories to U.S. newspapers. But many believe that a mine that would sink a battleship was far beyond their resources and skill. Others have speculated that a homemade bomb could have been planted on the hull of the ship. Two Americans at the scene said they heard a cannon blast.

Or could this amazing, state-of-the art ship have malfunctioned? Many of the ships built after the Civil War had problems with the coal bunkers overheating. The coal bunkers fueled the ship. When one overheated, a fire could start. A fire could eventually cause an explosion. The *Maine* was equipped with an alarm letting the sailors know if the temperature reached too high of a level. The alarm never went off.

The *Maine* was towed out into deep water and sunk. Was this a conspiracy led by the United States government, who decided to go to war against Spain without any hard proof? Was the U.S. afraid of finding out the truth in future years? It appears that this mystery will continue to remain unsolved.

The Plan for the *U.S.S. Maine* Play

Directions: Your group will be working together to write and perform a play about the explosion of the *U.S.S. Maine.* Use the questions below to help you organize your play. Remember, your play should convince others of this viewpoint.

Who was responsible for the explosion aboard the *Maine*?_____

Each person in your group will need to participate in your play. Write the names of the characters

in your play and describe each one. _____

_____

_____

_____

What is the setting of your play? _____

How will you show who is responsible for the explosion in your play? _____

_____

Give a brief outline of the play:

Beginning:_____

_____

Middle: _____

_____

Conclusion: _____

_____

A Letter to George Preston Blow

Directions: In the space below, write a creative letter to the man who survived the explosion on the *Maine*, George Preston Blow. In this letter, you should explain your opinion on the explosion and give good reasons for your opinion. In fact, you are trying to convince Mr. Blow of your opinion.

Dear George Preston Blow,

Teacher Lesson Plans

Standard/Objective

✸ Identify and use processes important to reconstructing and reinterpreting the past, such as using a variety of sources; providing, validating, and weighing evidence for claims; checking credibility of sources; and searching for causality. (NCSS)

✸ Acting as detectives, students will question suspects in the Lindbergh Baby kidnapping case and create a profile of the possible culprits.

Materials

copies of *Attention Grabber* (page 77); copies of *Lindbergh Comic Strip* (page 78); copies of *Background Information* (pages 79–81); copies of *Graphic Organizer* (page 82); copies of *Lindbergh House Plans* (page 83); one copy of *Character Cards* (page 84–86); copies of *Ransom Notes* (page 87); copies of *The Comic Solution* (page 88)

Discussion Questions

✸ What crime has been committed?

✸ Who was the crime committed against?

✸ When and where did the crime take place?

✸ Why would someone commit this crime against a celebrity like Charles Lindbergh?

✸ In your opinion, what kind of person would commit a crime like this?

The Activity: Day 1

Before students come into the classroom, hang wanted posters (page 77) all over the room for students to see. In addition, write these words on the board: "Police Headquarters." Welcome your students by calling them deputies and announce that they have a case to solve. Give students time to study the wanted poster. Then ask the discussion questions above. Create a list on the board for the last question. Students might want to add or take away from this list as they continue to make a profile of the culprit or culprits. Tell students that they will be acting as police deputies as they listen to evidence and then create a profile of the person or persons who committed this crime.

Teacher Lesson Plans *(cont.)*

The Activity: Day 1 *(cont.)*

Distribute *Lindbergh Comic Strip* (page 78) to students and let them read it silently. Then give the students *Background Information* (pages 79–81). Let them break into small groups and read it aloud. Then distribute *Graphic Organizer* (page 82). Have students use the background information to create profiles of these people involved in the case. Remind students that when creating a profile, they should only write down the important information about that person or anything that might help them with cracking the case. After each student has written his or her profile, have students group back together and share their profiles. At this point, students can add or take away information on their profiles. This profile page should be saved and added to as the week continues.

The Activity: Day 2

Distribute *Lindbergh House Plans* (page 83) for reference. Begin by telling students that they will be interviewing suspects and reviewing evidence the rest of the week. Choose four students and give them each a different character card from Day 2 (page 84). These students will be the suspects who will be interviewed today. Instruct students to read over the material silently and then read the material to the class, acting as a suspect. After each student presents his or her information as a suspect, let students work on a profile for that suspect.

Teacher Notes: To make them more durable, you may wish to copy the character cards on pages 84–86 onto cardstock and laminate them.

The Activity: Day 3

Distribute copies of *Ransom Notes* (page 87) for reference. Ask students to work up a profile of the suspect by simply looking at these notes. What can they infer about the suspect by his writing? They should notice that he has trouble with spelling. Some might even say that he is a foreigner.

Teacher Note: It was clear to investigators that the writer was not American-born because of his language. Basic words were misspelled, while difficult words were correct. It was possible that the criminal was one person, even though the ransom notes said "we."

Choose five students and give them each a different character card from Day 3 (page 85). These students will be the suspects who will be interviewed today. Instruct students to read over the material silently and then read the material aloud to the class acting as a suspect. After each student presents his or her information as a suspect, let students work on a profile for that suspect.

Teacher Lesson Plans *(cont.)*

The Activity: Day 4

Choose three students and give them each a different character card from Day 4 (page 86). These students will be the suspects who will be interviewed today. Instruct students to read over the material silently and then read the material aloud to the class acting as a suspect. After each student presents his or her information as a suspect, let students work on a profile for that suspect.

Lastly, present the following questions to the students:

* ❋ Did police set up Hauptmann because he matched the description, or was he the kidnapper?
* ❋ If he was involved, did he act alone?
* ❋ What about Violet Sharpe?
* ❋ What about the reference Cemetery John made to Condon about Betty Gow and Red Johnson?
* ❋ What about the other half of the ransom money that never turned up?

Let students discuss these questions in small groups.

The Activity: Day 5

Tell students to review their profiles and notes on the case. Who do they think committed the crime? Remind students of the comic from the first day. Tell students that they will be creating the comic that solves the case. Distribute *The Comic Solution* (page 88). Have students create the final comic page for the newspaper that solves the crime. Then, as a final activity, have students voice their opinions about the solution by reading their comic strips to the class. Display these comics for all to see.

Attention Grabber

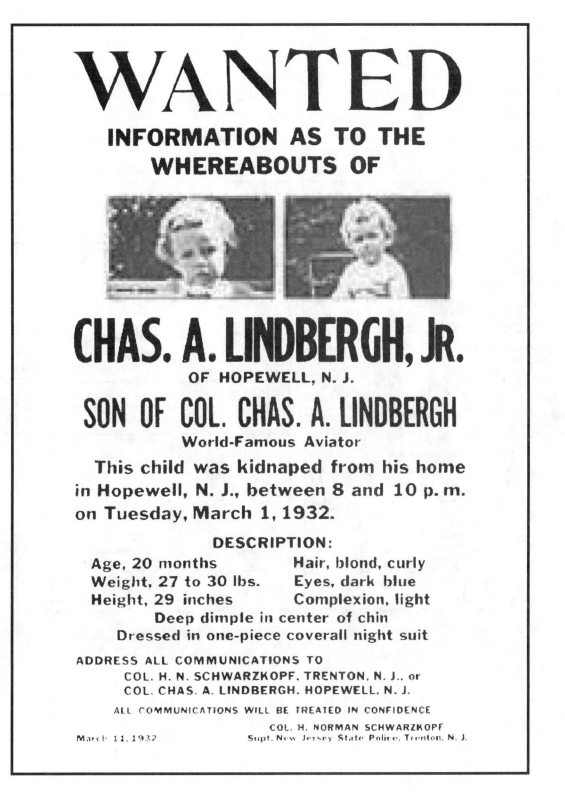

Lindbergh Comic Strip

Not all comic strips were funny during the Great Depression. This is one example of how a paper in New Jersey told the story of the Lindbergh kidnapping. Each week, a new scenario was printed in the paper to inform the public of the recent developments on the case.

THE CRIME OF THE CENTURY

CHARLES A. LINDBERGH BECOMES AN INTERNATIONAL HERO AFTER HIS FAMOUS FLIGHT TO PARIS. HE RETURNS TO A HERO'S WELCOME IN NEW YORK.

TO ESCAPE THE CROWDS AND THE PRESS, "LUCKY LINDY" HAS A SECLUDED MANSION BUILT IN THE SOURLAND MOUNTAINS IN HOPEWELL, NEW JERSEY.

HIS WIFE AND NEWBORN SON ARE HAPPY, UNTIL...

ON THE NIGHT OF MARCH 1, 1932 A SHADOWY FIGURE ENTERS THE NURSERY

AT TEN O'CLOCK HIS WIFE'S SCREAMS BRING MR. LINDBERGH RUNNING. THERE IN THE NURSERY IS AN EMPTY CRIB AND A LETTER ON THE WINDOWSILL

THE LINDBERGH BABY HAS VANISHED.

Background Information

During the 1930s, when most of America was suffering from the poverty of the Great Depression, some people turned to crime (like kidnapping) to get money. At this time there was one wealthy man who emerged as the most famous man in the world. He was famous for being the first to fly an airplane from New York to Paris. He was America's hero. His name was Charles Lindbergh, and his wealth and fame made him a target. His son was kidnapped and held for ransom.

Lindbergh was married to Anne Morrow. On June 22, 1930, she gave birth to their first child, Charles Lindbergh Jr. The family wanted privacy from reporters. They had two residences on large pieces of land. During the week, they stayed at the in-laws' estate, called Next Day Hill. On weekends the family lived at their own estate near Hopewell, New Jersey. Their house had 20 rooms. They hired a staff consisting of a butler, Olly; his wife, Elsie; and a nursemaid, Betty Gow. These two houses were 50 miles from each other.

The weekend before the crime, the Lindbergh family had gone as usual to the Hopewell house. By Monday, the baby had gotten a cold, so Anne decided to stay at Hopewell instead of returning to Next Day Hill. On Tuesday, March 1, 1932, the baby appeared to be better, but Anne was not feeling well. She called Betty Gow at Next Day Hill and asked her to come to Hopewell to help her with the baby. Betty came that afternoon. They prepared the baby for bed that evening and dressed him in warm clothes. Anne attempted to close all the shutters on the windows in his room, but the shutters on the corner window were too warped to close all the way. Betty was the last to leave the room, at 7:30 P.M., and she cracked the window open to allow the air to circulate.

About 15 minutes before Charles Lindbergh arrived home, Anne thought she had heard a car in the gravel driveway. She looked but didn't see anything, and the dog had not barked. Charles Lindbergh arrived home around 8:30 P.M. and had dinner with his wife. Around 9 P.M. Lindbergh believed he heard a sound similar to a wooden orange crate breaking. He thought it came from the kitchen on the right side of the house. Around this time Betty received a call from her boyfriend, Henry "Red" Johnson. They had planned to go out that evening but had canceled their plans when Betty was called to Hopewell.

more to follow

Background Information *(cont.)*

Around 10 P.M. Betty went up to the nursery to check on the baby before going to bed. She closed the window and turned on the electric heater. At first she panicked when she did not hear the baby breathing, but then she noticed that he was no longer in his bed. She ran into Anne's room and asked if she had the baby. Anne suggested that Charles maybe had the baby, and Betty quickly made her way into the library to find him. Both Charles and Anne went to the nursery to find it unusually cold. The corner window (remember, the shutter wouldn't close all the way) was open. Just under the window, on top of the heater, was an envelope. Charles waited for the police to arrive before touching it. He knew his baby had been stolen.

At 10:25 P.M., Olly called the sheriff's office to report the crime. Lindbergh called his attorney, Henry Breckinridge, and the New Jersey State Police Department. The local deputies arrived first and examined the floor in the nursery. Clumps of mud were found inside the nursery around the window. Footprints were found outside the nursery window. The footprints measured larger than a man's size 9 shoes.

The criminal had evidently worn a bag or sock over his shoe to prevent making distinct shoe prints in the mud. A carpenter's chisel was found outside directly underneath the window. The footprints led them 75 feet away, where there lay a homemade wooden ladder. This ladder was uniquely made, with the rungs very far apart. The side railing on one section had split apart. The ladder had three sections that fit together to make it reach 20 feet high.

The state police chief, Norman Schwarzkopf, arrived at 10:55 P.M. By 11:00 P.M. the police had set up a roadblock, hoping to catch anyone suspicious traveling with a child. The house was searched. No fingerprints were found inside the nursery on the window ledge or heater—not even the prints of Anne or Betty. No prints were found on the chisel or the ladder. Lindbergh was questioned as to why his dog had not barked at the intruder. He explained that the dog slept on the other side of the house and would not have been disturbed by someone trying to be quiet.

Background Information *(cont.)*

Olly told police that he had sent a man and woman away after they drove up to the house in a green car earlier that day. The woman was seen later hiding behind a bush trying to take a picture of the nursery window. On Tuesday two men in a black car had been asking people in the area for directions to the house. The car was traced to a man in New York who had reported it stolen that very day. At midnight, a woman with a child and two men were spotted at a train station in New Jersey. They looked very nervous, but they were never identified.

Police had many questions to grapple with. First, why wouldn't the kidnapper wait until everyone was asleep before taking the baby? This would have given him or her more time to get away. Why hadn't the dog barked? Was it because the culprit was a member of the house? The criminal had a chisel, so police believed that he or she did not know the shutter would be open. The baby's blanket had not been moved, so police believed the baby was pulled out of the bed by his head. No chloroform was noticed in the air, but police did not rule out the possibility that the baby had been drugged to keep him quiet. The fact that the kidnapper knew the location of the baby's room was not a surprise: during its construction, this house had been featured in magazines all over the country, along with its floor plans.

At first many believed that the mob was behind the crime. Al Capone, a famous gangster behind bars, was so offended by the accusation against the mob that he offered $10,000 for any information leading to finding the criminals. Schwarzkopf believed the criminals were from the local area and not professionals because of the fairly small ransom request. Another detective believed it was an inside job by one of the household employees. The family never spent Tuesday nights at Hopewell, and only the servants and the grandparents knew they would be there. However, both Charles and Anne refused to believe it was one of their servants.

Meanwhile, ransom notes were delivered to the Lindberghs. Each of these had a distinct signature with interlocking circles. It was the sign to identify the kidnapper.

Graphic Organizer

Directions: Write a brief profile of the person under each name.

Charles Lindbergh

Anne Morrow

Betty Gow

Olly

Elsie

Henry "Red" Johnson

Lindbergh House Plans

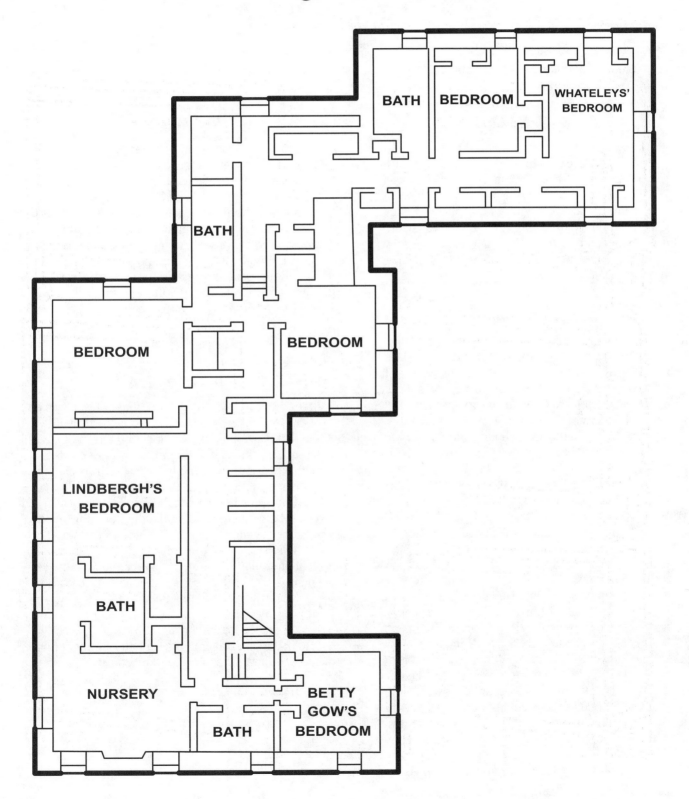

Character Cards

Day 2

Directions: Distribute these character cards to various students in the classroom. No one should receive the same card. Instruct the students to act as the character when questioned by police. All the information should be told to the deputies.

Betty Gow

I knew the whereabouts of the baby, and I also had direct access to him. Before working for the Lindberghs, I had a job in Detroit. There is a mobster named Scotty Gow who also lives in Detroit. He is known for kidnapping. Police have worked hard trying to figure out if I had any connections with this mobster, but so far they haven't found any evidence to support this theory.

Violet Sharpe

I am another servant for the Lindbergh family. I usually stay at Next Day Hill. My coworkers describe me as friendly and a good worker. I have a steady boyfriend named Septimus Banks. He is the butler and the main servant in charge of Next Day Hill. I think we will get married someday. The day of the kidnapping, I answered the phone call for Betty Gow. It was Mrs. Morrow. Before leaving for the Lindbergh home, Betty told me that the baby was sick and would not be returning to Next Day Hill that day. When I was interviewed by the police, I was very nervous and agitated. I didn't like them prying into my personal life. I told them that on March 1 at 8 P.M. I received a call from a man who I had met while taking a walk the weekend before. He offered me a ride home, and then asked me to go out. On March 1, this man and another couple took me out to the movies. I don't remember the name of this man, and I don't remember what movie we saw. I also can't remember the name of the couple who went out with us. When the police checked my bank account, they found that I had $1,600 in the account. I only make $100 a month, and most of that is sent home to my family back in England. It is possible that I saved all that money if I was extremely frugal. My hostility made police very suspicious.

Red Johnson

I am Betty's boyfriend. I also knew where the baby was on March 1 because Betty had to break a date with me. When the police picked me up, they found out that I had a green Chrysler coupe. This was a problem, because a local resident said that he had seen a green car near the Lindbergh house on the day of the crime. Inside my car the police found an empty milk bottle in the seat. I told them that I drink lots of milk and that I usually toss the empty bottles in the backseat. I've never had a criminal record, but I am an illegal alien.

John Condon

I am 72 years old. I was once a gym teacher and a principal of a school. I just wanted to do something to help the Lindberghs, so I ran an ad in the newspaper offering to act as a go-between. The day after the ad ran in the paper, I received a letter that had the interlocking circles. The Lindberghs believed the letter to be authentic because the media and public did not know about the special signature with circles that the kidnapper used. After showing the Lindberghs the letter, they agreed to let me be the go-between man. We ran the ad saying "Money is Ready" on March 11. I used the nickname "Jafsie" to protect my identity. The following day I received a phone call from a man with a thick accent. He had a taxi driver deliver a letter to my home. We decided to meet.

Character Cards *(cont.)*

Day 3

Joseph Perrone

I am the taxi driver who delivered an envelope to the address of John Condon on the evening of March 12. I told police that a man wearing a brown coat and a brown felt hat had given me the envelope. I also told police that this man had a thick German accent. I noticed that he wrote down my license plate number as I was driving off with the envelope.

Cemetery John

No one knows my name, but since I met with John Condon in a cemetery, they call me Cemetery John. Condon noticed that I was wearing the brown coat and hat, just as the taxi driver had seen. Condon also noticed that my voice was the same as the man on the telephone. I told Condon that I worked with a kidnapping gang consisting of four men, with one of the men being a high-level government worker. I also told him that Betty Gow and Red Johnson were not a part of the crime. I assured Condon that the baby was well and that I would send proof that we really had the baby. I sent the baby's sleeping suit.

Dr. Erastus Mead Hudson

I am a doctor and an independent fingerprint expert. I was called in to see if I could lift anymore fingerprints in the nursery and on the ladder. I was able to lift 500 partial prints from the ladder. Most of these were unusable. By this time, many people had handled the ladder.

Violet Sharpe

The police questioned me again on April 13. I was just as hostile this time as I was when they first questioned me. I suddenly remembered that I had not gone to the movies on March 1 but instead had gone to a restaurant called the Peanut Grill. The man's name was Ernie. He knew that I worked for the Lindberghs, but that is all. Police also found out that my sister had applied for a visa to return home to England on March 1, the day of the kidnapping. She left the country on April 6 without telling police.

John Condon

Lindbergh paid the $50,000 in ransom money on April 2. I delivered it to Cemetery John. He told me that the child was on a boat with two women. The women were innocent. He gave the location as being just off the coast of Martha's Vineyard. Lindberg immediately got in his plane and searched the waters. There was no boat in sight. Lindbergh and everyone else knew that the kidnapper had outsmarted him.

One hope remained: the police had recorded the money's serial numbers. In this way, they hoped to trace the money to the kidnapper as it was spent.

Character Cards *(cont.)*

Day 4

William Allen

I am a 46-year-old truck driver. On May 12 I was driving near the Lindbergh home at Hopewell, when I needed to go to the bathroom. I stopped alongside the road and walked into the woods. After walking about 70 feet, I saw a small skull and a leg sticking out from the ground. The body was identified as the Lindberg baby. The medical examiner said that the baby died on the night of the kidnapping. It seemed that he died from a blow to the head. Police speculated that the baby had been accidentally dropped against the house when the ladder split from the weight of the kidnapper.

Violet Sharpe

I was questioned again and again by police. I checked myself into a hospital and believed I was going crazy. Police found six business cards in my room with the name Ernie Brinkert. When shown his picture, I identified him as the man I went out with on March 1. I had no idea why his cards were in my bedroom. Not long after, I was found dead. I killed myself by drinking poison. Why did I do this? Police know I did not kidnap the baby. I was with the other servants at Next Day Hill. Did I unknowingly help someone else pull off the kidnapping by providing information? You will never know for sure. When questioned by police, Ernie Brinkert denied ever knowing me. In June a man named Ernie Miller told police that he was the man who took me out. His story collaborated with the second story I told police. The other couple also told the same story to police. Why did I identify Brinkert in a photo? He looked nothing like Miller. Miller did not know.

Bruno Richard Hauptmann

By late summer some of the bills began showing up in New York. The police began tracking where these bills were found. Bank tellers remember the man to be medium tall, with blue eyes, high cheekbones, and a pointed chin. In addition, the man wore a hat and spoke with a foreign accent. Then a bill showed up at a gas station. The worker was suspicious that this bill was a counterfeit, so he wrote down the man's license plate on the bill. The license number belonged to me, a German born carpenter. When police arrested me, they found a $20 bill with the right serial numbers. They also took many of my notebooks, which had sketches of ladders. The taxi driver, Joseph Perrone, identified me in a lineup as the man who gave him the envelope. But John Condon refused to ID me. In my garage was found more than $11,000 of ransom money matching the serial numbers. I told police that a man named Isidor Fisch gave this money to me. Fisch had returned to Germany a few months before and had died. Before leaving the U.S., he asked me to hold on to his belongings. One day I opened a box and found the money and decided to spend it. Fisch owed me money, and I took it upon myself to take it back. I must also tell you that after I was arrested, the ransom bills stopped showing up. About half of the ransom money was never found. I told police that I did not know anything about the kidnapping. One detective said that a piece of wood used as a rung in the ladder was taken directly from a floorboard in my attic. I maintained my innocence up to the end. It appeared to me that police had tampered with evidence in my attic where the supposed board came from. Also, they tampered with my time sheets from my work. That was my alibi on March 1. Nevertheless, I was tried and convicted of the crime. I died in the electric chair in 1936.

Ransom Notes

This first note was near the window in the nursery.

> Dear Sir! Have 50.000$ redy 25000$
> in 20$ bills 1.5000$ in 10$ bills and
> 10000$ in 5$ bills. After 2-4 days
> we will inform you were to deliver the
> Mony. We warn you for making
> anyding public or for notify the Police
> the child is in gut care. Indication for
> all letters are singnature and 3 holes.

Note to John Condon after seeing his advertisement in the paper on March 8.

> dear Sir: If you are willing to act as go-between in
> the Lindbergh case please follow strictly instruction.
> Handel incloced letter personaly to Mr. Lindbergh. It
> will explain everyding. don't tell anyone about it as
> soon we find out the press or Police is notifyd
> everyding are cancel and it will be a further delay.
> Affter you gett the mony from Mr. Lindbergh put
> these 3 three words in the New York American
>
> MONEY IS REDY
>
> Affter notise we will give you further instruction.
> don't be affrait we are not out fore your 1000$ keep
> it. Only act stricly. Be at home every night between
> 6-12 by this time you will hear from us.

The Comic Solution

Directions: You alone believe you know the solution to this crime. Complete this comic book with a comic strip that gives the solution in the squares below.

Teacher Lesson Plans

Standard/Objective

✻ Develop critical sensitivities, such as empathy and skepticism regarding attitudes, values, and behaviors of people in different historical contexts. (NCSS)

✻ Students will analyze the background information, maps, and time period and then write a newspaper article that reports the answer to the mystery of Amelia Earhart.

Materials

copies of *Attention Grabber* (page 92); copies of *Graphic Organizer* (page 93); copies of *Mapping Earhart's Journey* (pages 94–95); copies of *Background Information* (pages 96–97); copies of *Amelia Earhart News* (pages 98–103); copies of *News Leak 1* (page 104); copies of *News Leak 2* (page 105); copies of *Reporting on Amelia* (page 106); maps and globes

Discussion Questions

✻ What do you think these newspaper articles are about?

✻ What makes the headline interesting to the general public?

✻ Do you think you would like to read these type of newspaper articles?

✻ Which article would you be most interested to read?

✻ What makes the headline mysterious?

The Activity: Day 1

When students enter the room, begin announcing "Extra! Extra! Read All About It!" and distributing copies of *Attention Grabber* (page 92). Let students take a few moments to read the headline and the article titles on the page. Divide students into groups of four and ask the discussion questions above. Allow time for each group to discuss the answers.

Write the name "Amelia Earhart" on the board. Ask students what they know about this woman. Then let students discuss their ideas in their small groups. Take some time and let each group share what they know with the entire class. Record some of this information on the board around her name. Explain that the class will be working on a mystery surrounding her disappearance. It might be helpful to remind the students that Amelia Earhart became famous during the time of the Great Depression. Explain that life was very different for women back then. They did not hold prominent places in society at that time. Even so, Amelia Earhart made it easy for the public to love her and idolize her every move. It might also be helpful to remind students that Charles Lindbergh had just flown over the Atlantic Ocean during this time. People were crazy about flying.

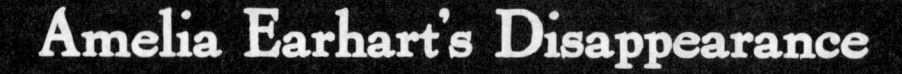

Teacher Lesson Plans *(cont.)*

The Activity: Day 1 *(cont.)*

Distribute *Background Information* (pages 96–97) and let students read the information in their small groups. Encourage students to add information to what was written on the board as they read this information. Distribute copies of *Graphic Organizer* (page 93) and have students write down all the things that they know about Amelia Earhart on this timeline. All recorded information should start with when she was born on one end of the line and then move to her disappearance on the other end.

The Activity: Day 2

Tell students that they will be reading real newspaper accounts of Amelia Earhart's journey. Make copies of *Mapping Earhart's Journey* (pages 94–95). Distribute this world map to students. Copy and distribute *Amelia Earhart News* (pages 98–103). Students will be taking these actual newspaper reports and tracking her journey beginning in Florida. Students can work in groups or individually to chart her course by these newspaper reports. Most students will need to look at other labeled maps and globes to complete this activity.

The Activity: Day 3

Tell students that they will be taking on the identity of newspaper reporters. Each of them works at a prominent newspaper in the United States. Have each student create a name for his or her paper. They can also create pen names for themselves. Explain that each reporter will receive a news leak that tells information about the mystery surrounding Amelia Earhart's disappearance. When they receive this information, they are to write a headline and a story to accompany it for their paper. Any background information that they might know about Earhart can be added, too. Students can also add a picture if they have time. Copy *News Leak 1* (page 104) and cut it into three sections. There are three news leaks on this page. Each student should receive only one news leak. Every student should take his or her news leak and write a newspaper headline and story about this news leak. This activity encourages students to develop their creativity. It does not matter whether the news leak can be proven or not. Explain to students that these are actual theories and stories about Amelia Earhart's disappearance.

Teacher Lesson Plans *(cont.)*

The Activity: Day 4

Have students' newspaper reports from the previous day posted around the class for students to read. Then tell students that there are other news leaks that will come to their attention today. Copy *News Leak 2* (page 105). Then cut the page in three sections so that only one news leak is on a section. Distribute one section to every student. Just like the day before, every student should take his or her news leak and write a newspaper headline and story about this news leak. This activity encourages students to develop their creativity. It does not matter whether the news leak can be proven or not. It is important for students to hear about all of these theories. This will help them decide on their theories for what happened to Amelia Earhart. Make sure there is time left at the end of class for students to share their stories and post them around the classroom.

The Activity: Day 5

Tell students that this is the day that each student will decide on his or her own theory about what happened to Amelia Earhart. Copy and distribute *Reporting on Amelia* (page 106). Students will be writing their own newspaper stories that include their theories of what happened to Amelia Earhart. These should be read aloud to the class. These newspaper stories will also make for a great discussion tool. Students can analyze these stories and divide them into categories.

Mysteries in American History

Attention Grabber

Graphic Organizer: Amelia's Timeline

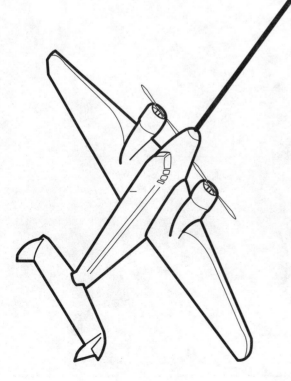

Mapping Earhart's Journey

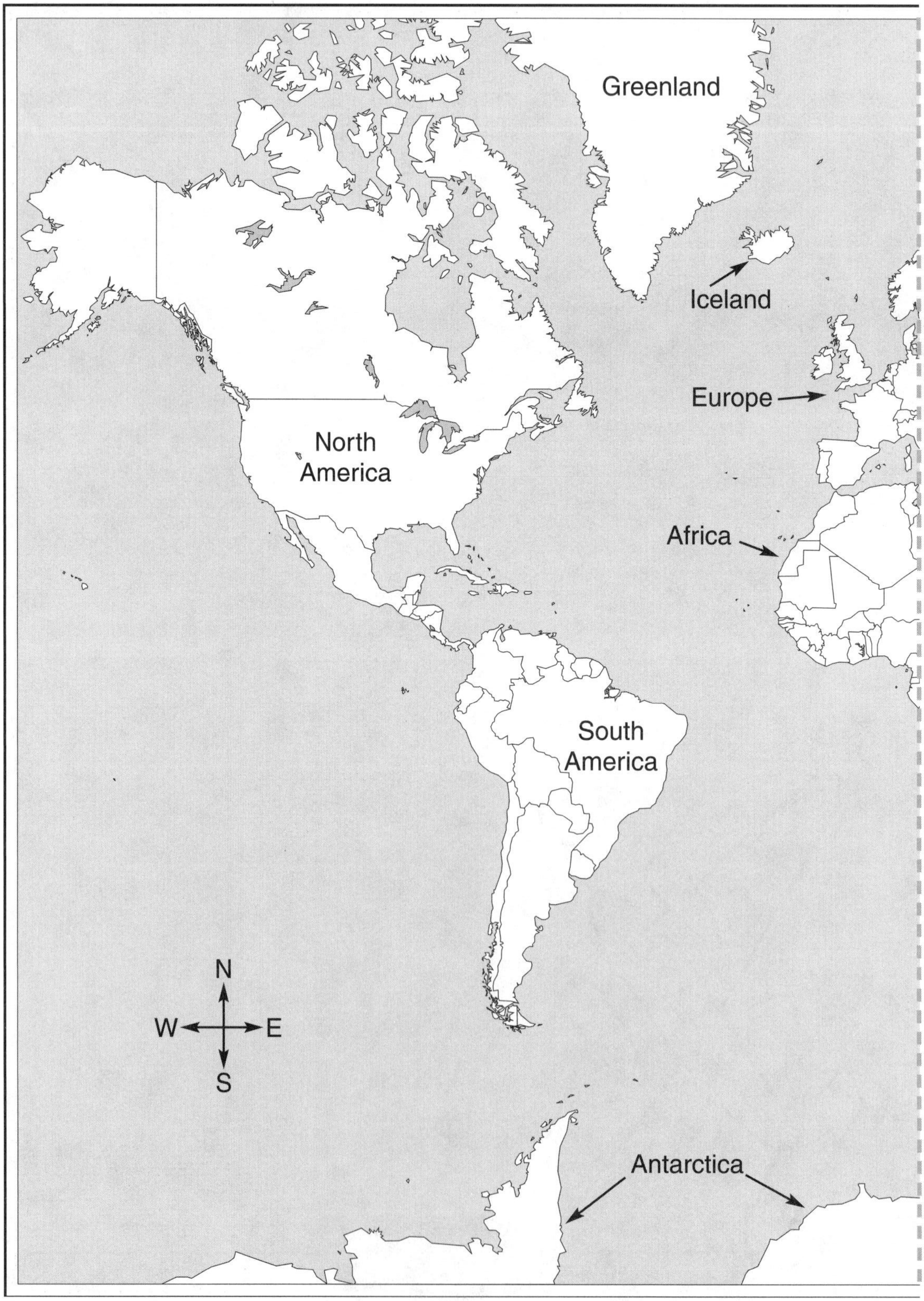

Greenland

Iceland

Europe →

North
America

Africa →

South
America

N
W ← → E
S

Antarctica

Mapping Earhart's Journey *(cont.)*

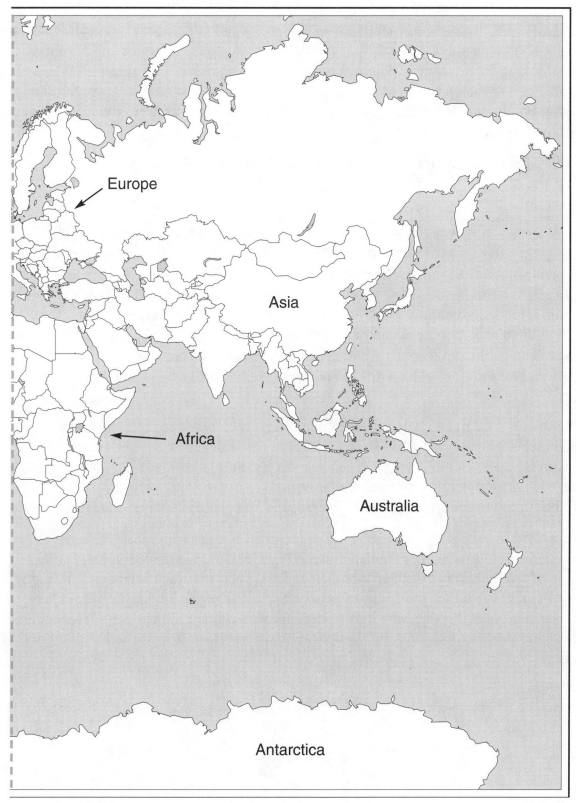

Background Information

She was called Lady Lindy because the public loved comparing her to Charles Lindbergh. Amelia Earhart was born on July 24, 1897, in a small town in Kansas. She grew up a tomboy and was always looking for adventure. She was a daredevil from the very beginning. When World War I came about, she enlisted as a volunteer nurse. For the first time in a war, airplanes were used to drop bombs and shoot at the enemy. Earhart was amazed at these flying machines and was determined to learn how to fly one.

She used her spare money to pay for flight instructions. She even bought her own plane. It was yellow, and she called it *Canary*. She began flying in 1920. She was a very fashion-conscious person. She bought a long leather coat and wore it to bed to make it look old!

In 1928 she received a call from a public-relations firm. They asked her to fly across the Atlantic Ocean to England on what they called a "goodwill flight." This flight was to represent the friendship between the U.S. and England. It was called the Friendship Flight. It was scheduled on June 18, 1928—exactly one year after Lindbergh's famous flight across the Atlantic. Earhart agreed to go on this flight, but she did not do any actual flying. Two other men actually flew the plane, and she accompanied them. She saw herself as just a passenger, a sack of potatoes. The public did not care. Earhart was a celebrity to them, and life was never the same for her. It was the time of the Great Depression, and Americans were always looking for heroes to give them hope.

Earhart used her celebrity status to help other women flyers. She was kept so busy with speaking engagements that she rarely had time to develop her skills as an aviator. Because of this, she had many accidents while flying. When she did fly, the fumes made her stomach upset. But this did not stop her determination. She vowed to break every record possible. It was especially important to Earhart to prove to herself that she could fly across the Atlantic alone.

Meanwhile, Earhart fell in love with a publisher named G. Putnam. He helped her with the publicity; she provided the celebrity connection he needed. Their marriage seemed to be happy for a while, but Putnam's need for money put stress on their marriage. Earhart even told her sister that she was tired of always hearing him complain about money. It was her trips, though, that kept them living the luxurious life. It was up to Earhart to do another profitable flight and make that money.

more to follow

Background Information *(cont.)*

Earhart began planning a trip that would set a record: flying around the world along the path of the equator. This flight would be 27,000 miles (43,000 km). She raised $80,000 to do the flight and even announced that aeronautical research would take place on the plane. She assembled a crew: two navigators and a stunt pilot who would act as an advisor. Earhart did not know how to use Morse code. She was not very good at using the two-way radio, either. The plane was equipped with both of these for safety reasons. To add to these complications, Earhart was worn out. She had traveled so much to promote this trip that she was suffering from severe exhaustion. She left on March 17, 1937, from California heading toward Hawaii. When she tried to land in Hawaii, she crashed on the runway. The plane was damaged, and they had to wait for it to be fixed. The flight had to be rescheduled.

Earhart never expressed fear on any of her previous flights, but she did on this one. She did not want to complete this flight. She only agreed to carry out this mission because of the contracts and all the money that was invested.

On June 1, 1937, her plane left Florida. Because of this delay, one of the navigators and the stuntman were not able to complete the trip. Only one navigator, Fred Noonan, was left to fly with Earhart. Like Earhart, Noonan did not know how to use the radio or Morse code. In fact, she left behind the Morse code key and the trailing wire antenna. To complicate matters more, Noonan was also known for drinking too much. On the previous trip, Earhart had to wake him up with lots of coffee to make him good at helping with the flight.

By the time her plane arrived in New Guinea in the South Pacific, she was not well at all. She sent cables to her husband telling him of her sickness. She left New Guinea for Howland Island. In the South Pacific, her plane entered a thick cloud. She could not see where she was going, and it hurt her navigation. She radioed her position to the U.S. Coast Guard on July 1. It was obvious that the clouds had blocked her view of her destination, Howland Island. She could not adjust the radio, and though the Coast Guard could hear her, she could not hear them. On July 5 a signal went out from her plane. After that she was never heard from again. Eight naval ships and 64 aircraft searched the area for 16 days hoping to find Earhart and Noonan and their plane. It was the largest and most expensive search in U.S. history. They found nothing. Her husband continued the search for two more years.

What happened to Amelia Earhart? Did her plane simply run out of gas? Did it crash, or did it land safely on an island? Did she survive? Did she want to escape from her stressed marriage and the pressure from the public? Or maybe Amelia Earhart was a spy. It was just before World War II, and the U.S. government was wondering about Japanese activity in the South Pacific. Maybe her disappearance gave the government an excuse to fly over the area and look for a Japanese military base. Neither her plane nor her body has been found. To this day, the mystery remains unsolved.

Amelia Earhart News

June 2, 1937

AMELIA FLIES ON

Miami, Fla., June 2—Pan American Airways reported that Amelia Earhart landed at Capripito, Venezuela, at 10:18 a.m., (Eastern Standard Time) today after a flight from San Juan, Puerto Rico.

It was expected that she and her navigator, Capt. Fred J. Noonan, would remain overnight in the Standard Oil company's guest house there and take off tomorrow for Paramaribo, Dutch Guiana. From there, she probably would fly to Natal by way of Uara, Brazil.

The aviatrix is flying around the world as near the equator as practicable, making the 28,000-mile journey for pleasure.

June 3, 1937

AMELIA IN GUIANA

Paramaribo, Dutch Guinea, June 3— Amelia Earhart landed here today at 12:50 A.M. (10:50 A.M. CST) on the third leg of her round-the-world flight.

The American woman flier set her heavy plane safely down after a flight of five hours and two minutes from Caripito, Venezuela.

She was expected to stay here until some time tomorrow.

June 4, 1937

AMELIA TO BRAZIL

Paramaribo, Dutch Guinea, June 4 — Amelia Earhart took off from here at 5:10 a.m., Eastern Standard Time, today on the fourth leg of her round-the-world flight.

Pan American airways, over whose route she has been flying since leaving Miami, Fla., reported that Miss Earhart was headed for Belem, in Brazil at the mouth of the Amazon river, a distance of about 820 miles from here.

The airways report added that she might try to reach Fortaleza, Brazil today for a hop of 1,628 miles. She will fly more than 900 miles over water crossing the mouth of the Amazon.

Courtesy of the Amelia Earhart Museum

Amelia Earhart News *(cont.)*

June 5, 1937

AMELIA POSTPONES HOP

Fortaleza, Brazil, June 5 — Amelia Earhart postponed her take-off here today to have her big round-the-world monoplane inspected.

She probably will remain over at least until tomorrow at this northeast Brazil port, 287 miles from Natal. After Natal, her goal will be Daka, Senegal, 1,900 miles across the Atlantic.

June 7, 1937

HOPE FOR AFRICA

Natal, Brazil, June 7 — Amelia Earhart headed over the South Atlantic in a light rain today for Daka, Senegal, her goal on the African continent in her intended flight around the world.

She left here on the 1,900 mile flight at 12:16 A.M. Central Standard Time and radioed more than four hours later that "everything is going fine."

June 8, 1937

AMELIA MAKES RECORD FLIGHT

South Atlantic Cross in 13 Hours, 22 Minutes

DELAYS HOPE ACROSS AFRICA

Slight Repairs and Adjustments Necessary Before Continuing Air Trip
Dakar, French Senegal, June 8 — Amelia Earhart flew here today from St. Louis, capital of Senegal, for an easier take-off on the next leg of her flight around the world.
Aviators here said Miss Earhart's time of 13 hours and 22 minutes for the 1,900 miles from Natal, Brazil, to Saint Louis, Senegal, where she landed yesterday, apparently was a record for the eastward South Atlantic crossing. The westward mark of 12 hours and 5 minutes also is held by a woman, Maryse Bastie. Miss Earhart flew through rain most of the way across the ocean, she said. The visibility at nightfall was bad and her wireless worked poorly.
The slim American flier laid up her plane here for repairs. She said it would be tomorrow or Thursday before she could hop off across Africa. She planned to follow the British route to Khartoum, in the Anglo-Egyptian Sudan, to avoid flying across the Sahara.
Miss Earhart disclosed she landed at St. Louis, 125 miles north of here because of bad weather. She decided to backtrack to Dakar, she said, because the airfield is more favorable for the takeoff than that at St. Louis.
Only slight repairs and adjustments were needed by her twin-motored monoplane, she indicated.

Courtesy of the Amelia Earhart Museum

Amelia Earhart News *(cont.)*

June 10, 1937

AMELIA IN AFRICA

Paris, June 10 — The air ministry announced that Amelia Earhart, flying around the world, landed at Gao, French West Africa, at 2:50 p.m. today, Greenwich Time (8:50 a.m. C.S.T.), after a hop from Dakar, Senegal.

Telegrams from the French military commandant at Gao to the ministry reported the American airwoman made a perfect landing after a flight of 7 hours 55 minutes.

Miss Earhart and her navigator, Captain Fred Noonan, told French authorities they would remain at Gao over night and take off tomorrow for Khartoum, Anglo-Egyptian Sudan.

June 11, 1937

AMELIA FLIES ON

Fort Lamy, French West Africa, June 11 — Amelia Earhart landed here today to complete a 1,000-mile leg of her flight around the world.

She set her twin-engined monoplane down at 6:55 a.m. (C.S.T.) after flying from Gao over equatorial Africa.

June 12, 1937

AMELIA IN SUDAN

El Fasher, Anglo-Egyptian Sudan, June 12 — Amelia Earhart, flying around the world, arrived here late today after a flight from Fort Lamy French equatorial Africa.

She expected to leave for Khartoum, also in the Sudan, at 5:30 a.m. local time Sunday (9:30 p.m. Saturday, Central Standard Time).

Miss Earhart landed here following a flight of about 900 miles from Fort Lamy. It is about 500 miles farther northeast to Khartoum.

She got a late start this morning, due to the necessity of adjusting the shock absorbers on her plane. They were damaged when she landed at Forty Lamy. She had planned originally to fly from Fort Lamy to Khartoum in one hop.

Courtesy of the Amelia Earhart Museum

Amelia Earhart News *(cont.)*

June 15, 1937

AMELIA IN INDIA

Karachi, India June 15 — Amelia Earhart arrived here tonight, completing a long and interrupted flight from Massawa, Eritrea, on her "just for fun" aerial flight around the world.

She had been reported for more than 29 hours on a leg of her flight that lay over Arabian desert and mountains and for about 1,000 miles across the Arabian sea.

Miss Earhart said she flew from Assab, Eritrea, on the African coast of the Red sea just north of the Gulf of Aden, to Karachi, on the Inrwan coast of the Arabian sea, in one hop. The airline distance is approximately 1,400 miles.

Miss Earhart said she would stay here probably a day but that her tentative plans to take off Thursday depended on the weather. Her itinerary, on the globe-girdling flight as close as practicle to the equator, calls for stops at Darwin, Australia, then across the Pacific to Oakland, Calif., by way of the Pacific Island route of Pan-American airways.

June 17, 1937

AMELIA IN CALCUTTA

Calcutta, India, June 17 — Amelia Earhart landed her round-the-world plane at DumDum airdrome here today after a 1,350 mile hope across Indian from Karachi.

Miss Earhart took off from Karachi at 7:25 a.m. Karachi time (7:55 p.m. C.S.T. Wednesday).

The flier, who is making a leisurely flight around the world "just for fun," said she intended to take off shortly after dawn Friday for Bangkok, capital of Siam. If she adheres to her planned itinerary, she will go from Bangkok, to Darwin, Australia, by way of Singapore, then Batavia, Dutch East Indies, and Surabaya, Java, before starting across the Pacific.

June 18, 1937

AMELIA DELAYED

Akyab, Burma, June 18 — Amelia Earhart started another leg of her round-the-world flight today after arriving from Calcutta, but bad weather forced her to return to Akyab.

She first landed her twin-motored monoplane at 12:34 p.m. (12:04 a.m. C.S.T.) after a 400-mile flight across the Bay of Bengal, and took off immediately in an effort to reach Bangkok, Siam. She was back in Akyab within two hours.

The flyer said she expects to start again for Bangkok early Saturday if the weather is favorable.

Miss Earhart left Dumdum airport just outside Calcutta at 7:05 a.m. Calcutta time (7:12 a.m. Thursday C.S.T.) despite reports of treacherous weather over the bay.

The airdrome had been drenched by monsoon rains and for a moment it seemed as though her plane would overturn as she left the waterlogged field.

Courtesy of the Amelia Earhart Museum

Amelia Earhart News *(cont.)*

June 19, 1937

AMELIA AT RANGOON

Rangoon, Burma, June 19 — Amelia Earhart reached Rangoon today after a 300-mile flight from Akyab on her leisurely globe-circling journey.

She landed her monoplane at 6:35 A.M. Greenwich time (12:35 A.M. C.S.T.) after a trip of two hours 53 minutes.

Her next destination was Bangkok, Siam, 400 miles southeast of Rangoon.

June 21, 1937

AMELIA TO REST

Bandoeng, Dutch East Indies, June 21 — Amelia Earhart decided today to take a three day rest and have her plane overhauled before taking off on the next leg of her flight around the world.

She landed at Bandoeng at 10:17 A.M. today (10:37 p.m. E.S.T.) after a flight from Singapore over the Java sea and a part of mountainous Java.

After her plane is checked she plans to take off for Darwin, Australia.

June 24, 1937

AMELIA PROCEEDS

Batavia, Java, June 24 — Amelia Earhart flew today from nearby Bandoeng to Sourabaya, Java enroute to Kupang, Timor Island, on her flight around the world. She planned to remain at Sourabaya, about 250 miles from Bandoeng, until tomorrow.

The flight ended a three-day rest.

Courtesy of the Amelia Earhart Museum

Amelia Earhart News *(cont.)*

June 30, 1937

AMELIA TO HOP

Aboard U.S. Coast Guard Cutter *Itasca* at Howland Island, June 30 — Amelia Earhart reported today she planned to start tomorrow on the most hazardous flight on her leisurely journey around the world.

The hop will carry her over 2,570 miles of ocean, from Lae, New Guinea, to Howland Island.

Because she crosses the international dateline she will complete the 18 or 20 hour flight a few hours before she starts it.

She radioed she will take off at 1:30 p.m. Thursday, Lae time, and expected to reach her goal between 10 a.m. and noon Thursday, Howland time. Translated into Central Standard Time, she will begin at 9:30 P.M. today and will land between 3:30 and 5:30 p.m. Thursday.

July 1, 1937

AMELIA HOPS TODAY

Oakland, Calif., July 1 — George Palmer Putnam announced that his flying wife, Amelia Earhart, would take off at 3:30 P.M. (Central Standard Time) today on the hazardous 2,570 mile flight from Lae, New Guinea, to Howland Island in her flight around the world.

Putnam said Miss Earhart possibly would complete the hop in 19 hours.

July 2, 1937

AMELIA NEAR GOAL

Oakland, Calif., July 2 — George Palmer Putnam reported today the coast guard cutter *Itasca* at Howland Island apparently had established communication with his flying wife, Amelia Earhart, en route from Lae, New Guinea, to Howland Island, a hop of 2,550 miles.

Shortly before 1 P.M. (C.S.T.) Putnam said Pacific shore stations reported inability to make radio contact with the *Itasca*. He took this to mean the cutter's wireless was busy "working Miss Earhart's world-girdling plane."

Putnam announced receipt of a message from the *Itasca*, at Howland Island, at 5:59 A.M. Saturday (11:29 A.M. Friday C.S.T.) indicating weather conditions there were almost ideal for a landing.

The slim American hopped off from Lae at 6 p.m. C.S.T. yesterday for the distant American-owned outpost. She said she hoped to reach there in 18 hours.

Her ultimate destination with her navigator, Capt. Fred Noonan, is Oakland. When she arrives she will have circled the globe "just for fun."

Courtesy of the Amelia Earhart Museum

News Leak 1

1. In the few years preceding World War II, the Japanese had taken over many islands in the South Pacific. Some believe Earhart was found by the Japanese and taken to Saipan, where she was held as a prisoner and possibly killed. The Japanese deny this theory.

2. Others believe that Earhart was a spy for the United States. They hold that the U.S. government sent her on this reconnaissance flight to learn more about Japanese activities on the Mandated Islands. It was wondered if the Japanese were building up a naval base there (which they were).

3. About 40 years later, a native woman on the island of Saipan said that when she was young, a foreign woman used to walk by her home. This foreign woman was tall with short, brown hair cut like a man's. Her hand and side looked to be burned. She stopped and gave her a ring. She found out that this foreign woman was staying in what they called the hotel and was heavily guarded. The native also noted that she remembered hearing about an airplane crash southwest of where she lived. The news had spread that the pilot was a woman.

News Leak 2

1. Another native woman said that she remembered that a woman had come to Saipan to spy and was caught and killed. A different woman heard about the crash while living on Saipan. The Japanese displayed the plane for all to see. They claimed it fell down from the sky, and the woman pilot had a special ring. Still others say they heard about a plane crash with a man and a woman aboard the plane.

✈ ✈ ✈ ✈ ✈

2. It is very possible that Earhart strayed off course, ran out of gas, and then crashed. Some even think that she crashed in the Marshall Islands. It is possible that after her crash she was able to send radio signals. The Japanese could have captured her and taken her to Saipan. There is an eyewitness account by a U.S. soldier stationed in Saipan who said that he saw her plane in a Japanese hanger.

✈ ✈ ✈ ✈ ✈

3. To this day, the search for Amelia Earhart continues. Expeditions to an island near Howland have turned up aircraft parts and a heel from a woman's shoe from the 1930s, but there is still no proof that they belonged to Earhart.

Reporting on Amelia

Directions: You, a local newspaper reporter, have solved the mystery! What happened to Amelia Earhart? Write your newspaper article in the space below. Be sure to include a catchy headline. If time permits, provide a picture, too!

Teacher Lesson Plan

Standard/Objective

* Identify and use processes important to reconstructing and reinterpreting the past, such as using a variety of sources; providing, validating, and weighing evidence for claims; checking credibility of sources; and searching for causality. (NCSS)

* Students will review the case against the Rosenbergs and decide their fate by writing the decision and sentence from a juror's perspective.

Materials

copies of *Attention Grabber* (page 110); copies of *Graphic Organizer* (page 111); copies of *The Prosecution's Evidence* (pages 112–113); copies of *Evidence: Venona Cable* (pages 114–115); copies of *Evidence: The Famous Sketches* (page 116); copies of *Vote* (page 117); copies of *The Defense's Evidence* (page 118); copies of *Persuasive Juror Speech* (page 119); copies of *What Really Happened in the Trial* (page 120); copies of *Sentencing the Rosenbergs* (page 121)

Discussion Questions

* Just because a person is convicted of a crime, does that mean he or she is guilty?

* What crime do you think has been committed?

* What qualities does an effective juror have?

* Do you think you are capable of being a good juror? Why or why not?

The Activity: Day 1

As students enter the room, give each of them a copy of *Attention Grabber* (page 110). (To make this seem very real, mail these letters to the students.) The attention grabber is a letter telling them that they have been summoned for jury duty. This letter should get students excited about reviewing a high-profile court case.

It is important that the teacher follows the instructions below in order to keep the students excited about this trial. They are not to know the outcome until day four. You are not allowed to give any additional information to the students, either.

Explain to students that the case is high-profile and concerns a couple named the Rosenbergs. Ask the discussion questions above. This can be done in small groups or in a classroom discussion. It is important for students to know the role of a juror. Have students work with a small group to write out possible answers to the third question above. Let students present their lists describing a good juror to the class.

Were the Rosenbergs Wrongly Convicted?

Teacher Lesson Plan *(cont.)*

The Activity: Day 1 *(cont.)*

Give students their jury instructions. They will be hearing the prosecution's case against the Rosenbergs first, and then the defense will present its case. Tell students that because they are jurors, they are not allowed to talk about this case to anyone, especially to the other jurors in this room. Remind students that jurors are not allowed to discuss the trial until both cases have rested. In addition, tell students that they are being sequestered for this trial. When a jury is sequestered, it means that they are not allowed to read the paper, turn on the news, or listen to the radio. For this jury, being sequestered means that they are not allowed to read any information about this trial (on the Internet, or in books, etc.). In addition, they are not allowed to talk about it with anyone outside this classroom.

Next, distribute *The Prosecution's Evidence* (pages 112–113) to the class and read this background information aloud. This is the prosecution's case against the Rosenbergs. Students are not allowed to ask questions, and they are not allowed to discuss this information. It is only to be read.

After reading the information, let students fill in *Graphic Organizer* (page 111). This organizer will help students to keep track of the many people involved in this spy ring and how they are related to one another. It will be used all three days of the trial.

Distribute *Evidence: Venona Cable* (pages 114–115) and *Evidence: The Famous Sketches* (page 116). Explain that this telegram was intercepted and decoded by the U.S. The key on the second page translates the code names into the names of the suspects. It may take a few minutes for students to understand how to read this cable. Then let students look at the sketches. These have been reproduced and reduced in size to allow all three to fit on a page.

Distribute the student page *Vote* (page 117). At the end of the class period, let students vote on whether they think the Rosenbergs are guilty or not guilty of conspiracy to commit espionage. This vote should be kept confidential. Collect these papers and keep a record of this vote.

The Activity: Day 2

Remind students of the jury instructions. Tell students that they will be reviewing more evidence from the case today. Since the prosecution has presented its case, the defense now has a turn to do the same. Distribute *The Defense's Evidence* (page 118). This information is the defense that was used for the Rosenbergs. Simply read the information aloud, but do not allow students to talk about the case or ask any questions. Let students fill in any additional information needed on their graphic organizers from the previous day. At the end of the class period, again distribute the student page *Vote* (page 117) and collect these papers. This vote should be kept confidential. Remind students of the vote totals from the day before.

Teacher Lesson Plan *(cont.)*

The Activity: Day 3

When students come into class, distribute the student activity sheet *Persuasive Juror Speech* (page 119). Remind students that after both sides have rested their case, the jurors finally get a chance to talk about the trial and find out how everyone feels. Tell students that they are to present a short (2–3 minutes) persuasive speech in front of their fellow jurors. This speech is meant to persuade the other jurors to their view. Each short speech should have evidence as its backbone. Give students a few minutes to prepare their speeches. Then let students hash out the case. Everyone should have a chance to present his or her speech. At the end of the class, take another vote (page 117). Then show students the vote totals from the previous two days. Ask students to reflect on how their vote has changed as more evidence has been presented. Then ask students to reflect on how their votes changed after talking with their fellow jurors. Although students have had a chance to talk about the trial, remind them that they are still sequestered to this jury room. This trial can only be talked about inside this classroom with other jurors. This lesson is not over yet.

The Activity: Day 4

Distribute *What Really Happened in the Trial* (page 120) to the students. Read this information aloud. Then distribute the student activity page *Sentencing the Rosenbergs* (page 121). Let students talk about what they have written. Show students the statistics from the previous days. End the class by asking the discussion questions again: "Just because a person is convicted of a crime, does that mean he or she is guilty? How does this apply to this case in particular and how it was tried in your classroom?"

Julius Rosenberg

Ethel Rosenberg

Attention Grabber

State of _____

County of _____

Jury Summons

JURY SUMMONS	**OFFICIAL DOCUMENT**
DO NOT DISCARD	

You are hereby summoned to be available as a trial juror for the _____ County Court.

Week of Availability   **Juror Number**

_____   _____

- -

RETURN THIS QUESTIONNAIRE PORTION WITHIN 5 DAYS OF RECEIPT

Name _____   Birthdate _____

Address _____

City _____ Zip Code_____ Phone _____

Have you ever been called to serve as a juror?	[ ] Yes	[ ] No
Have you or any member of your immediate family served as a witness?	[ ] Yes	[ ] No
Have you or any member of your immediate family ever been sued?	[ ] Yes	[ ] No
Are you either a close friend of or are you related to any law-enforcement officer?	[ ] Yes	[ ] No
Have you ever been convicted of a crime?	[ ] Yes	[ ] No

Graphic Organizer

Directions: Create a diagram in the blank box below. In your diagram, use the names listed to show how they are connected in this famous espionage case.

* Emanuel (Manny) Bloch

* Max Elitcher

* Alexsandr Feklisov

* Klaus Fuchs

* Harry Gold (Raymond)

* David Greenglass (soldier at Los Alamos)

* Ruth Greenglass

* Julius Rosenberg

* Ethel Rosenberg

* Morton Sobell

The Prosecution's Evidence

Julius and Ethel Rosenberg are on trial for espionage. This trial will decide if they spied for Russia, betrayed the United States, and exchanged documents that helped the Russians build an atomic bomb.

It begins in 1950 when Klaus Fuchs (fwooks), a scientist at Los Alamos, New Mexico, is arrested for spying. By this time the atomic bomb had already been created and used by the United States during World War II. Klaus Fuchs confesses that on two occasions he had passed secrets about the atomic bomb to a man named "Raymond." Fuchs is serving nine years in prison.

After finding Fuchs guilty, the FBI shifts their focus to a man named Harry Gold, the one suspected to be "Raymond." It takes only a week for Harry Gold to confess that he had met a soldier in Los Alamos, New Mexico. This soldier had given him a diagram of a lens. This lens was used to build the atomic bomb. Harry Gold is found guilty of espionage and is serving 16 years in prison. Gold agrees to help the government.

When shown pictures, Gold identifies the soldier who gave him the diagram. This soldier's name is David Greenglass. He said that Greenglass is the soldier he had met in Los Alamos.

The Prosecution's Evidence *(cont.)*

Greenglass admits he passed the diagram of the atomic bomb. He agrees to take the stand. During his testimony he points the finger of guilt at his sister, Ethel Rosenberg, and her husband, Julius. Greenglass claims that Julius Rosenberg first talked with him about spying for the Communists in 1943. In 1944, Greenglass started working as a scientist for the U.S. government in Los Alamos, New Mexico. He began providing top-secret information to Communist spies about an explosive lens used in the atomic bomb. He said that he turned over these top-secret sketches to both Julius Rosenberg and Harry Gold ("Raymond") at different times. David Greenglass, along with his wife, Ruth, testifies that Ethel was present during some of their meetings and even typed up some of the memos containing top-secret information. The government believes that Ethel helped her husband pass top-secret information to the Communists. She is being tried alongside her husband. Documents show that both Ethel and Julius were members of the Communist Party before they were married.

After the FBI arrested Julius, five different people who knew Julius Rosenberg suddenly either disappeared or were arrested. A man claims that he saw Julius trying to get passports for his family right before he was arrested. He remembers him by his unruly children. The government makes the case that the Rosenbergs were thinking of fleeing the country.

Max Elitcher, a friend of Julius Rosenberg, gives the most damaging evidence to the FBI. Max claims that Julius Rosenberg tried to recruit him into espionage work during the years of 1944–1948. Max says that while he shared the same political views as Rosenberg, he refused to spy for Russia.

Both Julius's and Ethel's attitudes on the stand were defiant. They refused to answer whether or not they had ever been members of the Communist Party.

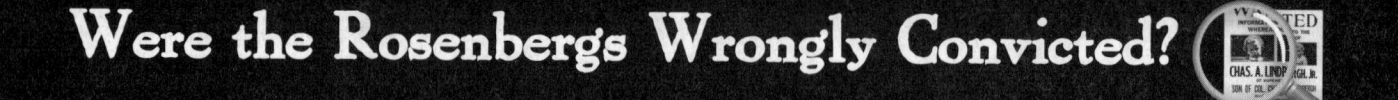
Evidence: Venona Cable

~~TOP SECRET~~ [word redacted] VENONA

[word redacted]

Reissue (T1362)

From: NEW YORK

To: MOSCOW

No: L347 (possibly)

21 September 1944

To VIKTOR [i]

Lately the development of new people [D% has been in progress]. LIBERAL [ii] recommended the wife of his wife's brother, Ruth GREENGLASS, with a safe flat in view. She is 21 years old, a TOWNSWOMAN [GOROZhANKA] [iii], a GYMNAST [FIZKUL'TURNITsA] [iv] since 1942. She lives on STANTON [STANTAUN] Street. LIBERAL and his wife recommend her as an intelligent and clever girl.

[13 groups unrecoverable]

[C% Ruth] learned that her husband [v] was called up by the army but he was not sent to the front. He is a mechanical engineer and is now working at the ENORMOUS [ENORMOZ] [vi] plant in SANTA FE, New Mexico.

[45 groups unrecoverable]

detain VOLOK [vii] who is working in a plant on ENORMOUS. He is a FELLOWCOUNTRYMAN [ZEMLYaK] [viii]. Yesterday he learned that they had dismissed him from his work. His active work in progressive organizations in the past was cause of his dismissal.

In the FELLOWCOUNTRYMAN line LIBERAL is in touch with CHESTER [ix]. They meet once a month for the payment of dues. CHESTER is interested in whether we are satisfied with the collaboration and whether there are not any misunderstandings. He does not inquire about specific items of work [KONKRETNAYa RABOTA]. In as much as CHESTER knows about the role of LIBERAL's group we beg consent to ask C. through LIBERAL about leads from among people who are working on ENORMOUS and in other technical fields.

Evidence: Venona Cable *(cont.)*

Your no. 4256[a]. On making further enquiries and checking on LARIN [x] we received through the FELLOWCOUTNRYMAN through EkhO [xi] a character sketch which says that they do not entirely vouch for him. They base this statement on the fact that in the Federation LARIN does not carry out all the orders received from the leadership. He is stubborn and self-willed. On the strength of this we have decided to refrain from approaching LARIN and intend to find another candidate in FAECT [FAKhIT] [xii].

MAJ [xiii]

No 751

20 September

~~TOP SECRET~~ [word redacted] VENONA

~~TOP SECRET~~ [word redacted] VENONA

Notes: [a] Not available.

Comments:

[i] VIKTOR: Lt. Gen. P.M. FITIN.

[ii] LIBERAL: Julius ROSENBERG.

[iii] GOROZhANKA: American Citizen.

[iv] FIZKUL'TURNITsA: Probably a member of the Young Communist League.

[v] i.e. David GREENGLASS.

[vi] ENORMOZ: Atomic Energy Project.

[vii] VOLOK: [word redacted]

[viii] ZEMLYaK: Member of the Communist Party.

[ix] CHESTER: Communist Party name of Bernard SCHUSTER.

[x] LARIN: Unidentified.

[xi] EkhO: i.e. ECHO, Bernard SCHUSTER.

[xii] FAKhIT: Federation of Architects, Chemists, Engineers, and Technicians. See also NEW YORK's message no. 911 of 27 June 1944.

[xiii] MAJ: i.e. MAY Stepan APRESYaN

28 April 1975

~~TOP SECRET~~ [word redacted] VENONA

Evidence: The Famous Sketches

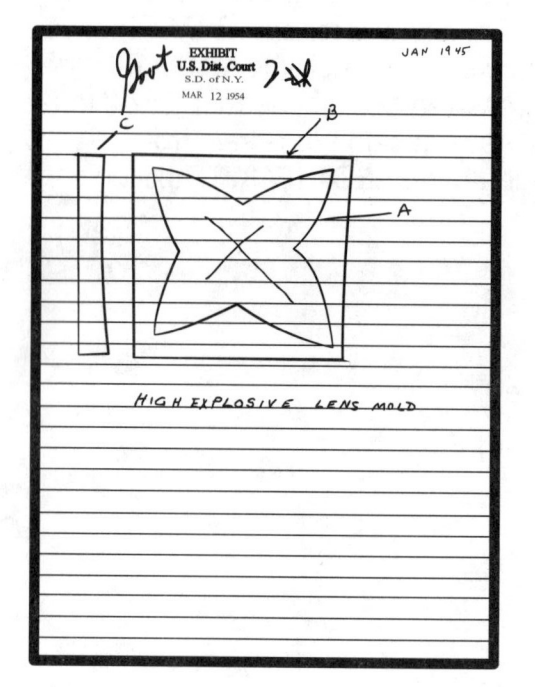

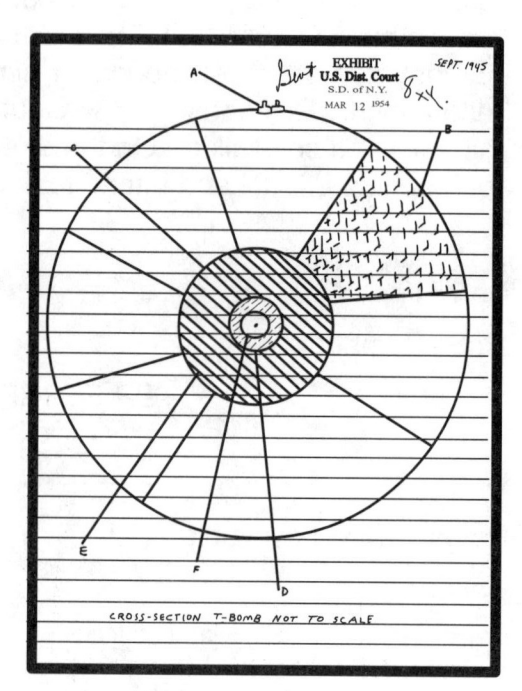

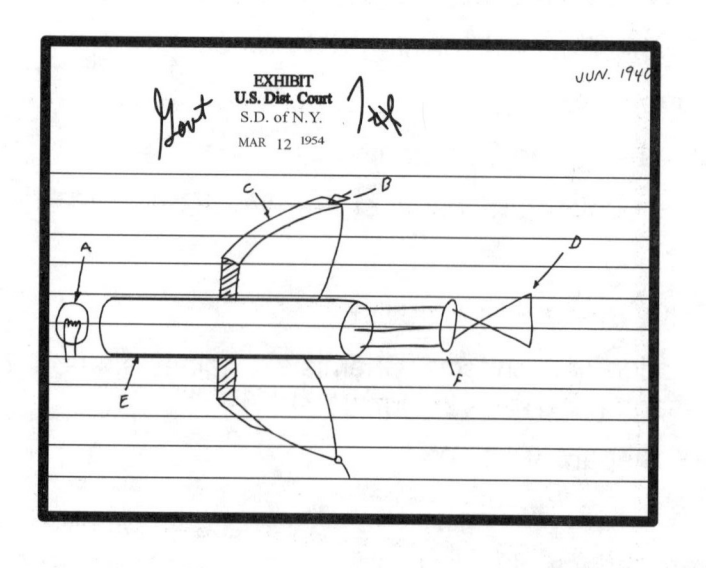

Vote

Directions: You have heard evidence today concerning the Rosenberg trial. If you had to decide their fate right now, would they be guilty or innocent? Record your vote in the space. Then write your specific reasons below your vote.

The Defense's Evidence

Julius is arrested at his home in front of his wife and two small children. He is handcuffed and taken away, and the house is searched. One month later his wife is arrested and not allowed to return home to tell her children goodbye and arrange for someone to keep them. They are ages three and five.

During FBI questioning, David Greenglass also points the finger of guilt at his wife, Ruth. Greenglass cut a deal with the FBI: Greenglass agrees to testify against his sister and brother-in-law. His wife is pregnant at this time. In return, the FBI promises not to charge his wife and give him a shorter prison term. During courtroom questioning, Greenglass appears to be very nervous.

When Julius Rosenberg refuses to admit any guilt, the FBI finds a way to arrest his wife, Ethel.

The government's evidence against Ethel is based only on the testimony of Greenglass and his wife, Ruth. Ethel testifies in court that her brother made up his story. He has always been known for lying and blowing stories out of proportion. She said that he was bitter over a bad business deal with Julius. Her brother had evidently lost a lot of money in the deal.

While Max Elitcher's testimony gives the most damaging evidence to the FBI, some believe he is scared into making up his story to avoid going to prison himself.

The Rosenbergs stopped going to the Communist meetings and taking the Communist paper the year before they were suspected of spying. They simply wanted to be together more as a family and didn't have time for the activities of the Party.

The Rosenbergs lawyer is Emanuel (Manny) Bloch. While this lawyer has done all he can, he has not represented them well. Not many lawyers would have wanted to defend anyone accused of being a communist during the Cold War, much less a spy for Communist Russia.

It does not help the Rosenbergs' case when they are asked about being communists. During the Great Depression, many people in the United States became very poor. Because of this, many young people in the U.S. joined the Communist Party. This was the case with the Rosenbergs. They saw communism as a way to take money and divide it equally between everyone, including the poor. Communism also provided workers with support by forming unions. The unions protected the workers. During World War II, Communist Russia was a friend to the U.S. With the blessing of the U.S. government, Hollywood made movies praising this communist country. After the war, however, the differences between the U.S. and communist countries like Russia created a large rift. It was not a good time for anyone to be accused of being a communist or a communist sympathizer in America.

The government believes they can pressure Julius into admitting that he spied if they threaten to sentence both Julius and Ethel. They believe Julius will cave in and tell them he was guilty of spying. In no way would a man want his children to be without any parents.

Persuasive Juror Speech

Directions: After both sides have rested their case, you, the jurors, finally get a chance to talk about the trial and find out how everyone feels. You are to present a short (2–3 minutes) persuasive speech in front of your fellow jurors. This speech is meant to persuade the other jurors to your view. Each short speech should have evidence as its backbone. Write your speech in the space below.

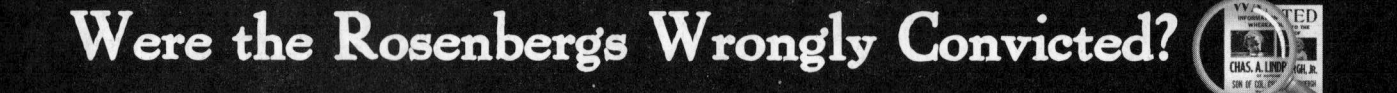

What Really Happened in the Trial

You should know these things about the time:

❋ The Cold War lasted over 40 years.

❋ It was a "war" between capitalist countries (U.S.) and Communist countries (Russia).

❋ It was called the Cold War because there was no direct fighting.

❋ Many U.S. citizens suspected of being Communists were put on trial.

❋ It was not a time in the U.S. when people could simply believe and do what they wanted in terms of political beliefs like Communism.

The government tried and convicted both Ethel and Julius of conspiracy. After their conviction and before deciding the sentence that they would serve, the judge secretly met with the prosecution lawyer (something that is not allowed without the defense lawyer being there, too). Both Ethel and Julius were sentenced to death for treason, even though they were not convicted of treason. This death sentence was unconstitutional.

The Rosenbergs appealed their case all the way to the Supreme Court. The chief justice and the U.S. attorney general met secretly (also something not allowed) and decided that they would not overturn the verdict. The day they were to be executed, a phone was placed in the jail with a direct line to the FBI. The government told Julius that if he confessed, he and his wife would not be executed. Even knowing that his two boys would be left with no parents, Julius refused to admit any guilt. He said, "Human dignity is not for sale."

Another friend of Julius was Morton Sobell. Sobell was convicted at the same time of the Rosenbergs and served 18 years in prison. To this day, he maintains that he and the Rosenbergs were innocent of spying for Russia. He firmly believes that Max Elitcher was pressured into making up a story for the FBI to avoid being tried for espionage.

In 1995, the U.S. government released 49 decoded telegrams that were intercepted between the U.S. and Russia back during the 1940s. These telegrams appear to say that Julius was an agent for Russia, but some (including the Rosenbergs' sons) believe these telegrams were "cooked" (meaning the government tampered with them). In addition, Russia will not confirm that Julius ever worked for them or gave information to their agents.

In 1997, a Russian agent named Alexsandr Feklisov told the public that Julius was one of his contacts. He said that the sketch Julius gave him was useful but not significant in helping the Russians build the atomic bomb.

Some believe that if the Rosenbergs could have stolen the plans for the atomic bomb, they would have done it. Others say that the Rosenbergs were wrongly convicted. Both Julius and Ethel died in the electric chair on June 19, 1953. This husband and wife were the only people put to death in the United States for spying during the Cold War.

Sentencing the Rosenbergs

Directions: Was justice served against the Rosenbergs? Were they both spies working against the government of the United States? Or did the government wrongly convict Ethel and Julius?

Imagine you were really a member of the jury during the trial of Ethel and Julius. What would you have decided about their case now that you have heard all the evidence? This is your chance to tell them what you would have done as a juror. Write your decision and their sentence (if given one) in the space below. Make sure you explain yourself and your opinion in detail.

Decision: _____

Sentence: _____

Explanation: _____

_____

_____

_____

_____

_____

_____

The JFK Assassination

Teacher Lesson Plans

Standard/Objective

❋ Identify and use processes important to reconstructing and reinterpreting the past, such as using a variety of sources; providing, validating, and weighing evidence for claims; checking credibility of sources; and searching for causality. (NCSS)

❋ Students will gather evidence about the Kennedy assassination while playing a game and then decide on a theory concerning the assassination.

Materials

copies of *Attention Grabber* (page 125); copies of *Background Information* (pages 126–128); copies of *Oswald Charged* (page 129); copies of *Graphic Organizer* (page 130); copies of *Witness Testimonial* (page 131); copies of *Kennedy's Route* (page 132); copies of *Evidence Cards* (pages 133–139); copies of *The Evidence Game* (pages 140–141); copies of *Oswald Speaks Out from the Grave* (page 142); game markers; dice

Discussion Questions

❋ What do you think about these coincidences?

❋ Do you think these coincidences really matter to investigators when collecting facts about the Kennedy assassination?

❋ What other coincidences can you think of between these two assassinations or any other two historical people?

❋ What is a conspiracy?

❋ Do you think Kennedy's assassination was covered up by the government? Why or why not?

The Activity: Day 1

Post the attention grabber (page 125) on an overhead projector. Have students take turns reading each point aloud. Tell students that this list is not the only mysterious thing about the Kennedy assassination. Ask the discussion questions above. Students might want to look up the word *conspiracy*. You can remind them that they talked about conspiracy in the Lincoln assassination lesson.

Teacher Lesson Plans (cont.)

The Activity: Day 1 (cont.)

Next, group students together to read the background information (pages 126–128). Let them discuss this information in their small groups and make a list of any questions that remain unanswered. Tell students that they will be deciding whether Oswald committed this assassination alone, as part of a larger group of assassins, or was completely innocent of this crime. Make copies of *Oswald Charged* (page 129) for students to view, as well. This document shows that the Dallas police charged Oswald with the crime.

Make a copy of *Graphic Organizer* (page 130) for students. (Each day, a new copy of this sheet will be given to students. All of these must be stapled together so that students can look back at how their opinion changes with each new piece of evidence.) Explain to students that they will be keeping a record of what they think about the evidence and the guilt or innocence of Lee Harvey Oswald. Have students record any outstanding evidence on this sheet under the appropriate title and explain why they feel Oswald is guilty, innocent, or just a patsy. Then divide the class in half. Label one side "Guilty" and the other side "Innocent". Tell students to walk to the side of the room that represents what they believe about Oswald and his involvement in the assassination. Students who walk to the middle of the room believe that he was involved in a conspiracy but did not actually assassinate Kennedy alone.

The Activity: Day 2

Distribute copies of *Witness Testimonial* (page 131) to each student. Explain that a reporter who was in the crowd the day that Kennedy was assassinated wrote this article. Her name was Mary Woodward, and she wrote for the *Dallas Morning News* newspaper. This article was printed the day after the assassination. Read this together as a class. Let students discuss how this article makes them feel. How do they think people would react today if our president were assassinated in the same way?

Distribute copies of *Kennedy's Route* (page 132) so that students can have a visual of the area where Kennedy was shot. They can refer back to the background information for added help from the day before, too.

Teacher Lesson Plans *(cont.)*

The Activity: Day 2 (cont.)

Tell students that they will gather evidence by playing a game. Have students form groups of four or five to play this game. Give each group one game board (pages 140–141) and one set of the evidence cards (pages 133–139). Have each student select a marker for his or her game board. Some might use a penny or an eraser. Each group will also need a die to roll. First, have each player roll the die to determine the order of each player's turn. The person who rolls the highest number will go first. Then each player will roll the die at his or her turn and advance along the game board. When a player reaches a labeled place on the game board, he or she can choose to read an evidence card or to roll again. If a player turns over a card that he or she has already read, he or she may choose the next card in the pile to read. Only one card can be read at each location. Then the player must move on to another location. He or she can return back to that location after visiting another location and gathering more evidence. Players can start anywhere on the board and move in either direction. Some places have more evidence than others. Give students about 20 minutes to play the game

Distribute another copy of *Graphic Organizer* (page 130). Have students record their new evidence on this page and then decide Oswald's guilt or innocence. Let students staple this page on top of the one from the previous day. Then divide the class in half. Label one side "Guilty" and the other side "Innocent." Tell students to walk to the side of the room that represents what they believe about Oswald and his involvement in the assassination. Students who walk to the middle of the room believe that he was involved in a conspiracy but did not actually assassinate Kennedy alone.

The Activity: Days 3 and 4

Allow students to continue to play the game and gather more evidence. Then distribute another copy of the graphic organizer (page 130). Have students record their new evidence on this page and then decide Oswald's guilt or innocence and staple it on top of the others from the previous days. Then divide the class in half again. Label one side "Guilty" and the other side "Innocent." Tell students to walk to the side of the room that represents what they believe about Oswald and his involvement in the assassination. Day 4 will be the last day of playing the game. No more evidence can be collected after this day.

The Activity: Day 5

Students will be making their decision about Oswald on this day. Distribute copies of *Oswald Speaks Out from the Grave* (page 142). Have students write their conclusions to this mystery from the mouth of Oswald himself. Allow enough time for students to read this at the end of class. During this time, let students ask additional questions and discuss why they made their final conclusions about this case.

Attention Grabber

Lincoln and Kennedy Coincidences

1. Lincoln was elected in 1860, Kennedy in 1960, 100 years apart.

2. Both men were assassinated on a Friday and in the presence of their wives.

3. Each president's wife had lost a child while living at the White House.

4. Both men were killed by a bullet that entered the head from behind.

5. Lincoln was killed in Ford's Theater; Kennedy met his death while riding in a Lincoln convertible made by the Ford Motor Company.

6. Both men were succeeded by vice-presidents named Johnson who were southern Democrats and former senators.

7. Andrew Johnson was born in 1808 and Lyndon Johnson was born in 1908, exactly 100 years later.

8. The first name of Lincoln's private secretary was John; the last name of Kennedy's private secretary was Lincoln.

9. According to some sources, John Wilkes Booth was born in 1839. Lee Harvey Oswald was born in 1939—100 years later.

10. Both assassins were Southerners who held extremist views.

11. Both assassins were murdered before they could be brought to trial.

12. Booth shot Lincoln in a theater and fled to a warehouse. Oswald shot Kennedy from a warehouse and fled to a theater.

13. Both "Lincoln" and "Kennedy" have 7 letters.

14. Both "Andrew Johnson" and "Lyndon Johnson" have 13 letters.

15. Both "John Wilkes Booth" and "Lee Harvey Oswald" have 15 letters.

16. A Lincoln staffer named Miss Kennedy told him not to go to the theater; a Kennedy staffer named Miss Lincoln told him not to go to Dallas.

Background Information

On November 22, 1963, President John F. Kennedy paraded through downtown Dallas, Texas, in a motorcade. He was shot and killed in his convertible as many watched helplessly in the crowd. The car rushed to Parkland Hospital, just a few miles away. Doctors tried valiantly to save him. They couldn't. Within hours, the body was flown on Air Force One to the Navy Medical Center in Washington D.C. Americans mourned their president.

Some say that the Kennedy assassination is the greatest murder mystery of all time. Was Lee Harvey Oswald the lone killer of Kennedy? Was there a larger conspiracy that included Oswald? One question that is rarely asked, however, is this: did Oswald even commit the crime at all?

The government launched an investigation into the assassination of Kennedy. This investigation team was called the Warren Commission. In the past 40 years since this investigation, many have been asking questions about its findings. Some say the Warren Commission ignored key evidence. A few think that the new president, Lyndon Johnson, wanted the case closed before the next election. Others believe the government just wanted the case closed so that the American public could heal and get on with life. Is there any truth to these speculations?

What do we know about Lee Harvey Oswald? He worked in the School Book Depository at the time of the assassination. He was young, married, and had two little girls. Oswald was very intelligent. He served in the marines for three years and also worked for the Central Intelligence Agency (CIA). He was trained to speak Russian and lived in Russia for three years. It was in Russia that he met his wife, Marina. His ability to speak the language was so good that she thought he was a Russian, too. While there, he asked for citizenship but was denied. Questions remain as to why he did this and if he was working for the CIA at the time.

After moving to Dallas with his wife and children, he boarded in a home near the Texas School Book Depository. His wife and children lived 14 miles away with a friend. He went home every weekend to stay with his family. The night before the assassination, Oswald had a friend drive him to his house. This was a Thursday, so it was unusual for Oswald to go home. He told his friend that he was going home to get curtain rods so that he could hang curtains in his boarding house. His wife's friend said that Oswald was especially quiet that night. The next day he left behind his wedding ring and money. He carried a brown package about two feet long under his arm. When his friend asked him about the package, Oswald said it was the curtain rods. His friend talked about the excitement of the day with Kennedy coming to town, but Oswald seemed uninterested.

more to follow

Background Information *(cont.)*

Oswald was named the lone killer. The Warren Commission concluded that the shots came from the sixth floor of the Texas School Book Depository, where Oswald worked. They said that there were three shots and that all of them came from behind the motorcade from the sixth floor of the Texas School Book Depository.

The crowd had lined the streets looking for the president to make his way through Dealey Plaza. The Secret Service walked around his car. The route was planned by the Secret Service and published for all to see ahead of time. It was no mystery where the president would be and the route his car would take.

There is even a theory that the parade route was changed in the days leading up to the president's visit. Some people contend that the president's motorcade was originally intended to travel straight down Main Street. The revised route had the motorcade turning right onto Houston Street and then left onto Elm Street. If the original route had been followed, then the president's car would have never passed by the Texas School Book Depository (where Oswald was working) or the grassy knoll (where the "true" shooters might have been hiding).

Despite the fact that President Kennedy, a Northern liberal, was visiting Dallas, Texas, a Southern city, no military guards were in the crowd that day. It was determined that they were not needed. Dallas police officers were on their motorcycles. Just before the shots rang out, a Dallas police officer saw something that looked like a gun in a window in the Texas School Book Depository. He frantically yelled at the Secret Service, "Something's up there!" But they did not hear him. The president's car slowed down.

In less than 10 seconds, at least three shots rang out. The confused crowd watched as the president suddenly lurched forward and grabbed his throat. Then, those nearby gasped in horror as a bullet struck John F. Kennedy in the head, fatally wounding him.

Within 15 minutes of the crime, a description matching Oswald was given to Dallas police. No one knows who provided this description. Thirty minutes after the shooting, a rifle was found on the sixth floor of the Texas School Book Depository building and the window was open. The location of the window was a perfect shot from behind the motorcade.

Where was Oswald during that time? Minutes before the assassination, Oswald was seen in the lunchroom eating. The motorcade was six minutes behind schedule, but the public did not know that it was behind schedule. Ninety seconds after the shooting, a police officer went inside the building and saw Oswald in the lunchroom by himself. The lunchroom was on the second floor. Oswald appeared very calm to the police officer. The shooting was believed to have taken place on the sixth floor. Could Oswald have fired the shots and then returned to the lunchroom four floors below? Oswald left work and headed to his boarding house. He took his revolver and a jacket before leaving the house.

more to follow

Background Information *(cont.)*

What happened next is also a mystery. A man walking down the street near Oswald's boarding house killed a policeman. Two eyewitnesses described a man, but they were totally different descriptions. A different eyewitness claimed that there were two men and that they ran off in different directions. The bullet that killed the police officer could not be traced back to Oswald's revolver. Did Oswald kill that police officer? If he did, why did he do it?

The police finally caught up with Oswald in a movie theater. He was interrogated for hours, but no record exists of what was said in this interrogation. Oswald did say, "I haven't done anything to be ashamed of." He only admitted to hitting a cop in the mouth. The police officers said that his answers seemed very rehearsed. He was not given a lawyer. Oswald was put in four lineups. The other men in the lineups were dressed much better than Oswald. Some were many years older or had blonde hair. They did not choose anyone else for the lineup who looked anything like Oswald. Each person in the lineup was asked where he worked, and Oswald was the only one who worked at the School Book Depository. By this time the public knew the fired shots were said to have come from that location.

When police went to where his wife lived to search the house, they asked her if Oswald owned a gun. His wife said yes and took them to see it. She pointed to a rolled-up blanket in the garage. When the officer picked up the blanket, there was nothing in it. Did the gun on the sixth floor belong to Oswald? Remember the brown package he took to work that morning? When the rifle on the sixth floor was dismantled, it was three feet long. This is one foot longer than the package that Oswald carried to work that morning. Oswald could not have carried his gun in the package that morning.

The city manager of Dallas made the decision to transfer Oswald to a higher-security prison. He told the police department how to do it. They had promised the press that they would be able to take photos during the transfer. Some of the officers thought it would be best to transfer him secretly, but they had no say in the matter. When Oswald was brought out, a man stepped forward and shot Oswald. This man's name was Jack Ruby.

The JFK Assassination

Oswald Charged

On November 22, 1963, President John F. Kennedy was assassinated in Dallas, Texas. A homicide report confirms the nation's worst fears: the president has died. Lee Harvey Oswald has been charged with the murder.

The following information can be found on the homicide report issued on November 23, 1963, by the Dallas Police Department.

Last Name of Person Killed, First Name:

KENNEDY, John F. (PRESIDENT OF U.S.)

Race, Sex, Age:

w (white), m (male), 47

Offense as Reported (Crime):

MURDER

Residence of Person Killed:

Washington, D.C. (White House)

Place of Incidence — Street and Number:

Elm St. (approx. 150' W of Houston St.)

Day of Week:	Date of Incidence:	Time of Day:
Fri	11/22/63	12:30 PM

Pronounced Dead by Physician:

Dr. Kemp Clark, 1PM, Parkland Hospital

The following description was given in a section titled, "Details of Offense":

"The expired was riding in motorcade with wife and Governor John Connally, and his wife. Witnesses heard gun shot and saw the expired slump forward. More shots were heard and the expired fell into his wife's lap. Governor Connally was also shot at the time. Car in which they were riding was escorted to Parkland Hospital by Dallas Police Officers."

Graphic Organizer

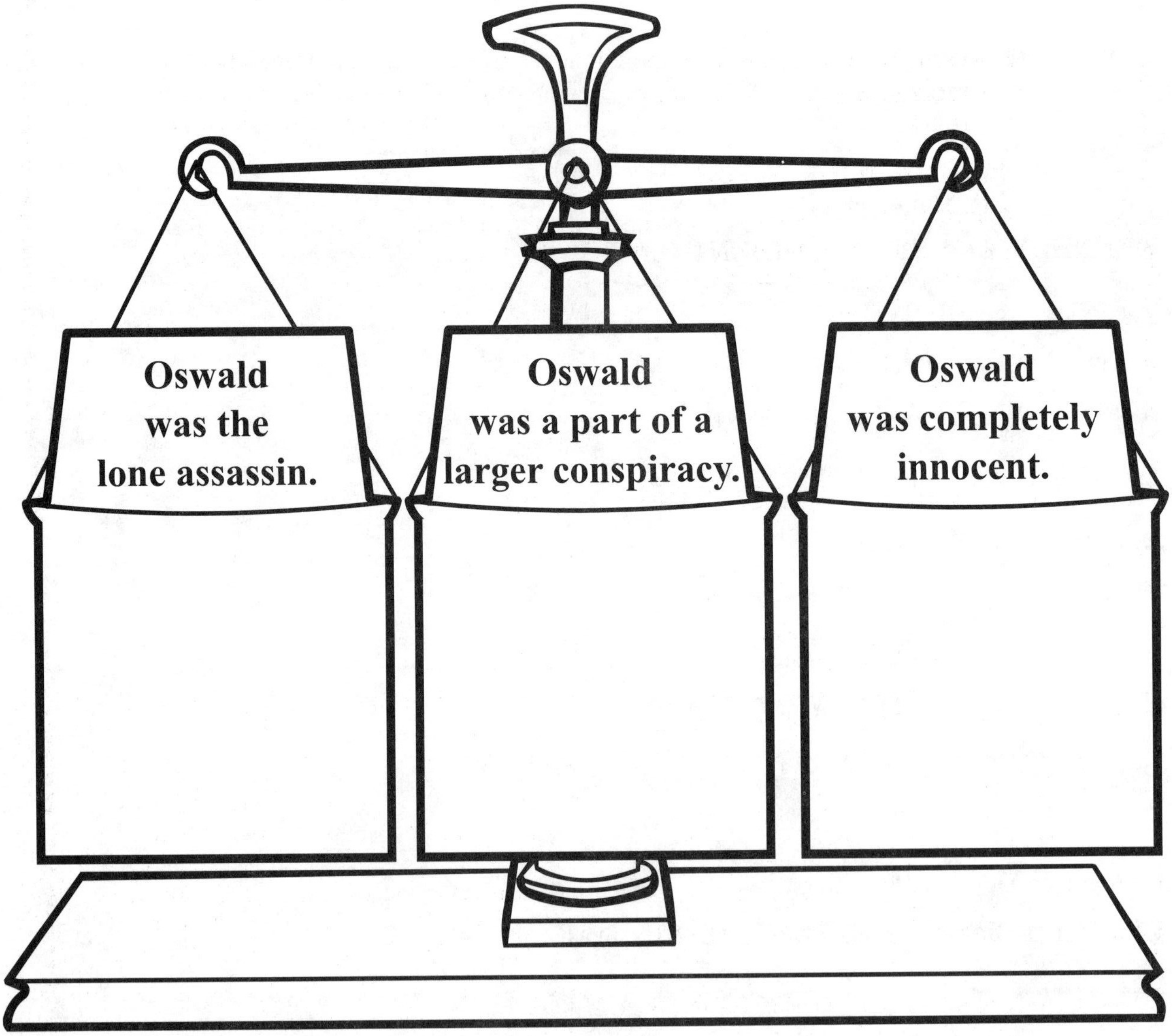

Oswald
was the
lone assassin.

Oswald
was a part of a
larger conspiracy.

Oswald
was completely
innocent.

Witness Testimonial

Witness From The News Describes Assassination

(The following eyewitness account was written by a Dallas News staff writer.)

by MARY E. WOODWARD

Four of us from Women's news, Maggie Brown, Aurelia Alonzo, my roommate Ann Donaldson, and myself had decided to spend our lunch hour by going to see the President.

We took our lunch along—some crackers and apples—and started walking down Houston Street. We decided to cross Elm and wait there on the grassy slope just east of the Triple Underpass, since there weren't very many people there and we could get a better view.

WE HAD BEEN waiting about half an hour when the first motorcycle escorts came by, followed shortly by the President's car. The President was looking straight ahead and we were afraid we would not get to see his face. But we started clapping and cheering and both he and Mrs. Kennedy turned and smiled and waved, directly at us, it seemed. Jackie was wearing a beautiful pink suit with beret to match. Two of us, who had seen the President last during the final weeks of the 1960 campaign, remarked almost simultaneously how relaxed and robust he looked.

As it turned out, we were almost certainly the last faces he noticed in the crowd.

AFTER ACKNOWLEDGING our cheers, he faced forward again and suddenly there was a horrible, ear-shattering noise coming from behind us and a little to the right. My first reaction, and also my friends', was that as a joke, someone had backfired their car.

Apparently the driver and occupants of the President's car had the same impression, because instead of speeding up, the car came almost to a halt.

Things are a little hazy from this point, but I don't believe anyone was hit with the first bullet. The President and Mrs. Kennedy turned and looked around, as if they, too, didn't believe the noise was really coming from a gun.

Then after a moment's pause, there was another shot and I saw the President start slumping in the car.

THIS WAS followed rapidly by another shot. Mrs. Kennedy stood up in the car, turned half-way around, then fell on top of her husband's body. Not until this minute did it sink in what actually was happening. We had witnessed the assassination of the President. The cars behind stopped and several men— Secret Service men, I suppose—got out and started rushing forward, obstructing our view of the President's car.

THEN I STARTED looking around at the stunned crowd. About 10 feet from where we were standing, a man and woman had thrown their small child to the ground and covered his body with theirs. Apparently the bullets had whizzed directly over their heads.

Next to us were two Negro women. One collapsed in the other's arms, weeping and uttering what everyone was thinking: "They've shot him."

It still seems like a horrible nightmare.

It will be a real-life nightmare to haunt us all for a long time to come.

Kennedy's Route

This is the route that Kennedy's motorcade took through Dealey Plaza in Dallas, Texas.

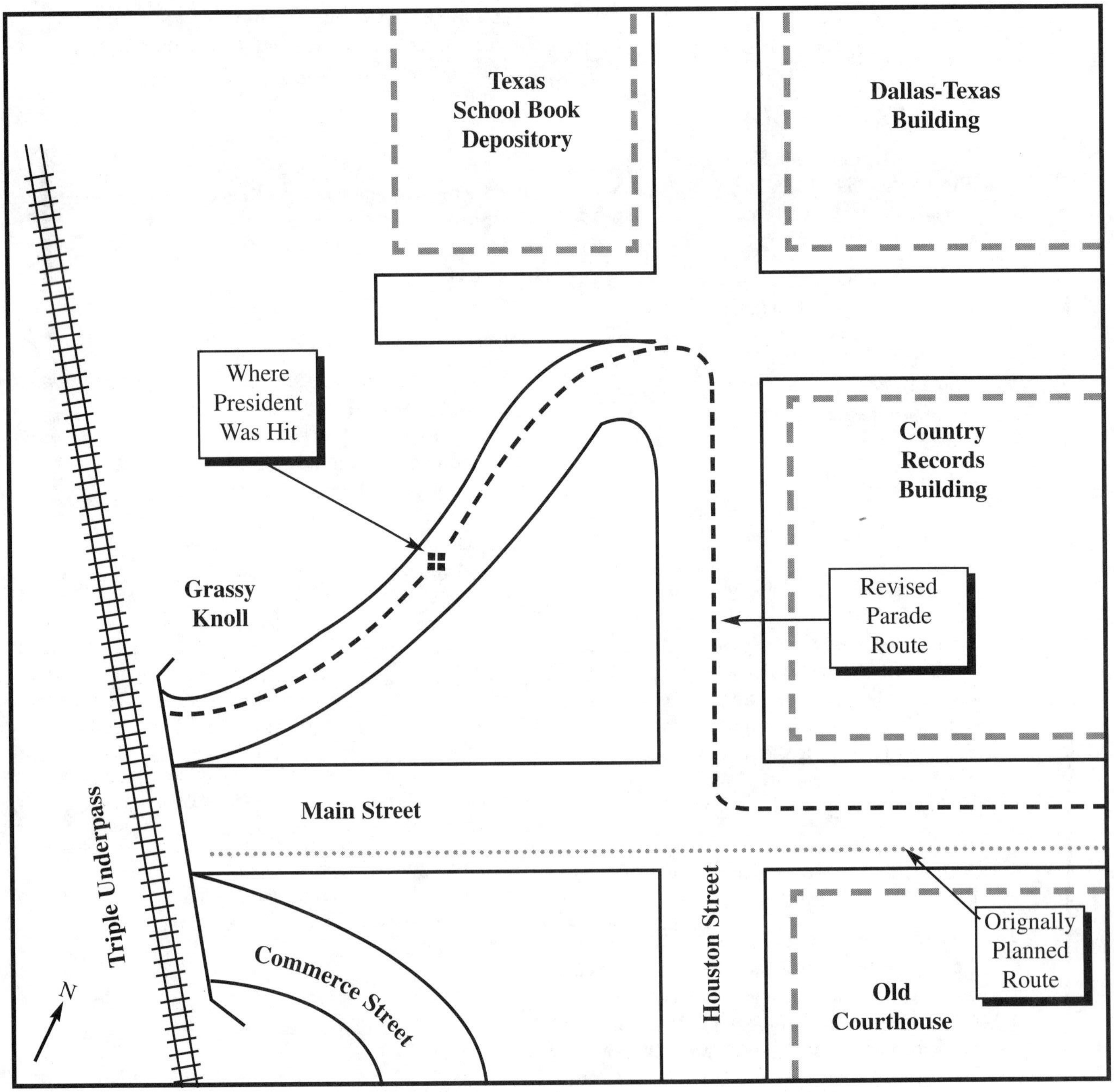

Texas School Book Depository

Dallas-Texas Building

Where President Was Hit

Country Records Building

Revised Parade Route

Grassy Knoll

Main Street

Triple Underpass

Houston Street

Orignally Planned Route

Commerce Street

Old Courthouse

N

Evidence Cards

Jack Ruby

The night before Oswald's transfer, the Dallas police received a phone call. The person on the other end said to change the plans on his transfer or Oswald will be killed. The officer who took the call knew the voice. He said the voice belonged to Jack Ruby.

Jack Ruby

Jack Ruby begged authorities to move the trial outside of Dallas during his testimony. They refused.

Jack Ruby

Jack Ruby had connections to the Dallas police. He owned a nightclub, and many officers went there.

Jack Ruby

Ruby contracted cancer and died while in jail.

Jack Ruby

Oswald was seen in Jack Ruby's nightclub two weeks before the assassination. After shooting Oswald, Jack Ruby was hysterical. When Ruby was told that Oswald was dead, he became suddenly calm. Ruby knew he would get the electric chair for this crime.

Jack Ruby

The Warren Commission never did explore the reasons behind Ruby killing Oswald. How did Ruby get into the police station to kill Oswald? Ruby claimed he got in through the basement on the ramp. A detective said that was impossible. He was guarding that ramp. He took a lie-detector test and passed it. Eight other witnesses said the same thing as the detective.

Jack Ruby

By April, Kennedy's trip to Dallas was planned, and Ruby began receiving calls from mob figures.

Evidence Cards *(cont.)*

The Grassy Knoll

There were 50 total witnesses on the grassy knoll who said the shots came from behind them.

The Grassy Knoll

A man standing on the grassy knoll said that a shot from behind went past his left ear and a second shot went over his head.

The Grassy Knoll

A nightclub singer named Beverly saw the figure of a person on the grassy knoll. There was smoke around that person. She had taken a picture of it, and a FBI agent took her undeveloped film. He promised that she would get it back. She never did.

The Grassy Knoll

A uniformed man with no hat and dirty hands took film from a man who was on the grassy knoll during the assassination. He never saw his film developed.

The Grassy Knoll

A photo taken by a woman shows a man on the knoll. This man was wearing a uniform that looked very much like a policeman's with a badge at the top.

The Grassy Knoll

A man reported that he saw two men, one a railroad worker and another wearing a uniform, behind the grassy knoll. Smoke was coming from their direction. He saw one of the men take a gun apart and place it in a tool box. The FBI offered him money to keep quiet about this.

The Grassy Knoll

A 22-year-old man by the name of Gordon was made to leave the parking lot behind the grassy knoll. The person who told him to leave was supposedly a CIA agent.

The Grassy Knoll

A man reported seeing two men behind the fence on the grassy knoll. One of them looked like a railroad signal man. The man who reported this died in a mysterious car accident two years later.

Evidence Cards *(cont.)*

The Zapruder Film

A man named Abraham Zapruder filmed Kennedy in the parade the day of the assassination. His film was 26 seconds long and showed the president as he was shot.

The Zapruder Film

The president was first seen grasping his throat after the first bullet was fired. Then his head went back and to the left as another bullet struck it.

Evidence Cards *(cont.)*

The Parkland Hospital

At Parkland, the doctors said the head wound showed the bullet came from the front as the back of Kennedy's head was blown off.

The Parkland Hospital

Doctors said that about 20–25% of Kennedy's brain was missing. An ambulance driver who transferred his body into the casket said that the back of Kennedy's head felt like a sponge and that his skull was missing in back.

The Parkland Hospital

Kennedy's body was placed in a very expensive casket. It was bronze with white satin lining. His head was wrapped in sheets.

The Parkland Hospital

The wound in the neck was very small and the doctors said it was an entrance wound. Therefore, the bullet came from the front.

The Parkland Hospital

The Secret Service did not allow doctors to perform an autopsy. They were with the doctors at all times.

Evidence Cards *(cont.)*

Naval Medical Center

When Kennedy's body was taken off the plane, he was in a different casket. The casket was plain and cheap.

Naval Medical Center

All of Kennedy's brain was missing. Therefore, it could not be sectioned out and examined.

Naval Medical Center

Kennedy's body was in a gray body bag.

Naval Medical Center

The wound in the neck was much larger than what the doctors had observed in Dallas. A few days later, the doctors who performed the autopsy were made to sign papers not to discuss Kennedy's autopsy with anyone, or else they would be court marshaled.

Naval Medical Center

The autopsy photos showed the back of Kennedy's head completely intact.

Naval Medical Center

The doctors performing the autopsy were not qualified to do it. They had no experience and were very young. During the autopsy, the Secret Service was in the room ordering the doctors around.

Naval Medical Center

The Warren Commission ignored the controversy over these photos. They also did not allow the doctors at Parkland Hospital to view the photos. Only the government had copies of the photos.

Naval Medical Center

Several items vanished from the National Archives: tissue slides from the autopsy and Kennedy's brain tissue. They were taken illegally and never returned.

Evidence Cards *(cont.)*

Oswald's Body at Rose Hill Cemetery

When Oswald was arrested, he had a fake identification card. The name listed was "Alex Hidell."

Oswald's Body at Rose Hill Cemetery

Oswald's wife had his body exhumed in 1981 to make sure his body was really there.

Oswald's Body at Rose Hill Cemetery

No prints were uncovered on Oswald's rifle until after his death. Then, a smudged palm print was discovered on the gun.

Oswald's Body at Rose Hill Cemetery

Oswald's casket had been disturbed. The vault was broken at the bottom, which shows that someone got into the casket.

Oswald's Body at Rose Hill Cemetery

When Oswald was in the operating room, Secret Service agents were there dressed to look like surgeons so that they would not stand out.

Oswald's Body at Rose Hill Cemetery

After two years, the experts said that the body was Oswald's. They based their evidence on his dental records. The mortician saw the skull and noticed that no autopsy had been performed. When someone has an autopsy, the skull is cut away at the top. The mortician knew that the man he buried 20 years earlier had an autopsy. He believes the head had been switched.

Oswald's Body at Rose Hill Cemetery

Secret Service agents went to the funeral home. They wanted to see the body alone. They fingerprinted and palm-printed Oswald. The funeral director noticed the ink after the Secret Service left.

Evidence Cards *(cont.)*

The Mob

Christian David, a foreigner and a drug smuggler, gave information to an American journalist in 1981. David told the journalist that he had been offered the contract in May 1963 to assassinate Kennedy. He turned the offer down because it was too risky.

The Mob

Christian David said that the bullets used were explosive bullets, which make a larger hole in the body. This type of bullet flattens out and cannot be traced.

The Mob

Christian David said that three men were hired to assassinate Kennedy. Two were a part of the mob in Marseilles. The other killer was a drug trafficker. One of these men wore a uniform the day Kennedy was shot.

The Mob

Christian David claims that four shots were fired: #1 hit Kennedy from behind, #2 hit the governor from the rear, #3 hit Kennedy from the front in the head, and #4 missed. Two of these shots were fired simultaneously.

The Evidence Game

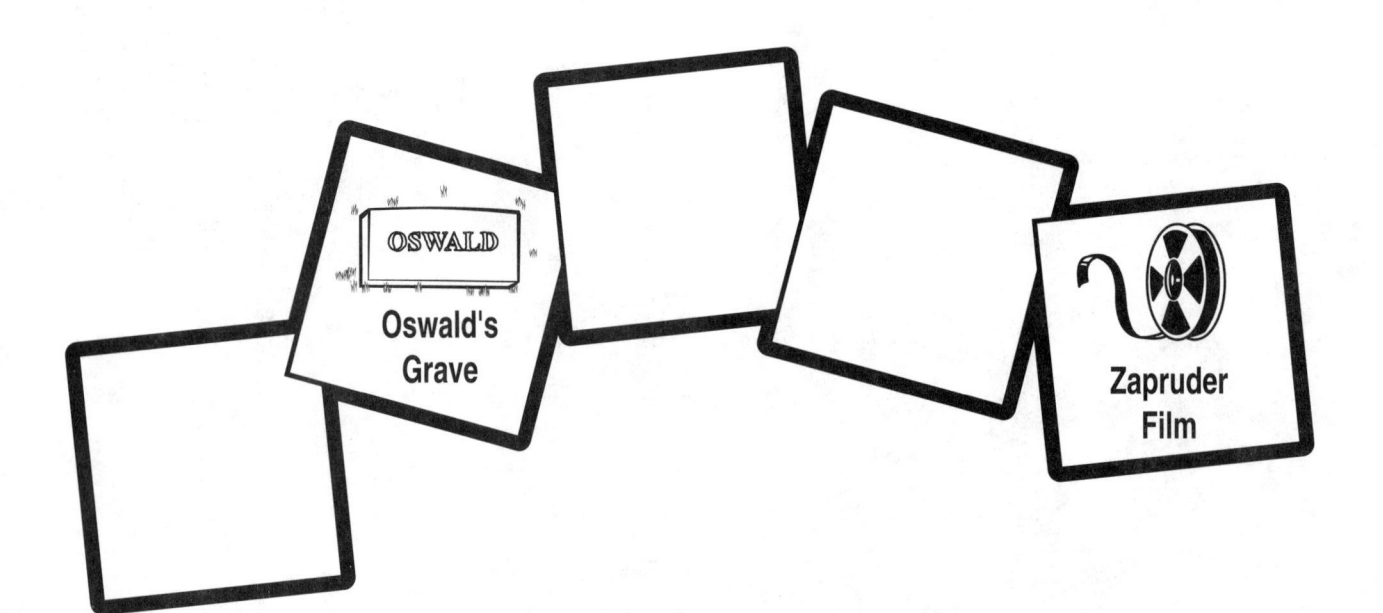

The Evidence Game *(cont.)*

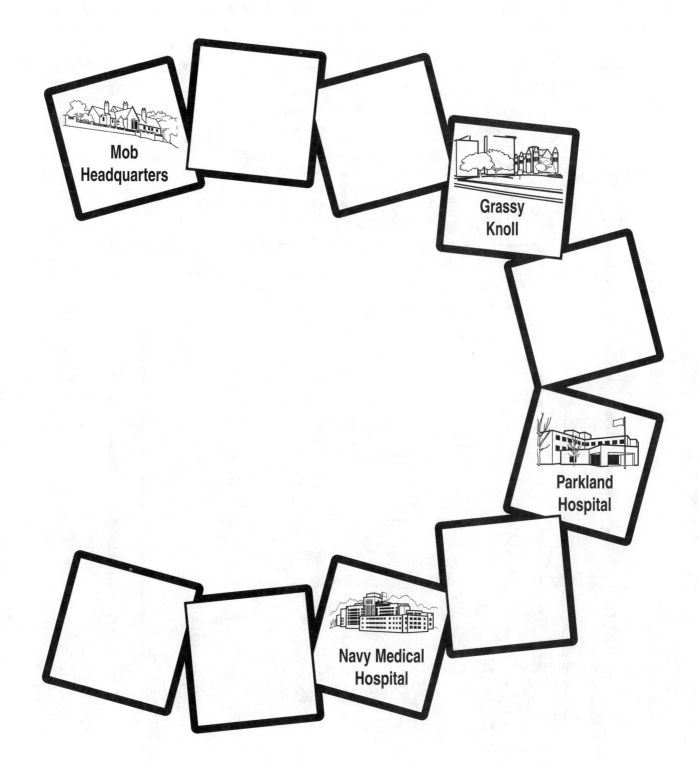

Oswald Speaks Out from the Grave

Directions: Was justice served to Lee Harvey Oswald? Did he alone assassinate President Kennedy? Was he a part of a larger conspiracy and simply used as a patsy? Or was Oswald completely innocent of this crime? Look at the evidence that you have collected. What if Oswald could speak out from the grave? In the space below, show what you believe by writing Oswald's words of truth about this crime.

HERE LIES...
...THE TRUTH

Bibliography

Books

Aronson, Marc. *Witch Hunt: Mysteries of the Salem Witch Trials.* Atheneum, 2003.

Blau, Melinda. *Whatever Happened to Amelia Earhart?* Raintree Steck-Vaughn, 1983.

Coleman, Brooke. *Roanoke: The Lost Colony.* PowerKids Press, 2000.

Donnelly, Judy. *Who Shot the President? The Death of John F. Kennedy.* Random House Books for Young Readers, 1988.

Goode, Stephen. *Assassination!: Kennedy, King, Kennedy.* Franklin Watts, 1979.

Hakim, Joy. *The First Americans.* Oxford UP, 2002.

Kimmel, Elizabeth Cody. *Before Columbus: The Leif Eriksson Expedition.* Random House Books for Young Readers, 2003.

Leder, Jane. *Amelia Earhart: Opposing Viewpoints.* Greenhaven Press, 1989.

Monroe, Judy. *The Lindbergh Baby Kidnapping Trial: A Headline Court Case.* Enslow Publishers, 2000.

Moss, Francis. *The Rosenberg Espionage Case.* Lucent Books, 2000.

Powell, Phelan. *Major Unsolved Crimes.* Chelsea House, 1999. Chelsea House, 1999.

Roach, Marilynne K. *In the Days of the Salem Witchcraft Trials.* Houghton Mifflin Co., 1996.

Roensch, Greg. *The Lindbergh Baby Kidnapping Trial: A Primary Source Account.* Rosen Publishing Group, 2003.

Rice, Earle Jr. *The Salem Witch Trials.* Lucent Books, 1996.

Sansevere-Dreher, Diane and Ed Renfro. *Explorers Who Got Lost.* Tor Books, 1992.

Schouweiler, Tom. *The Lost Colony of Roanoke: Opposing Viewpoints.* Greenhaven Press, 1991.

Somerlott, Robert. *The Spanish-American War: "Remember the Maine."* Enslow Publishers, 2002.

Waggoner, Jeffrey. *The Assassination of President John F. Kennedy: Opposing Viewpoints.* Greenhaven Press, 1989.

Walsh, John. *The Sinking of the U.S.S. Maine, February 15, 1898: The Incident That Triggered the Spanish-American War.* Franklin Watts, 1969.

Wilson, Lori Lee. *Salem Witch Trials: How History Is Invented.* Lerner Publishing Group, 1997.

Yolen, Jane. *Roanoke: The Lost Colony—An Unsolved Mystery from History.* Simon & Schuster, 2003.

Zeinert, Karen. *The Lincoln Murder Plot.* Linnet Books, 1999.

———. *The Salem Witchcraft Trials.* Venture Books, 1989.

Bibliography *(cont.)*

Websites

* **Salem Interactive Map**

  http://jefferson.village.virginia.edu/~bcr/salem/salem.html

* **Salem Witch Trial Transcripts**

  http://www.salemwitchtrials.com/transcripts.html

* **Salem Witchcraft Trials**

  http://www.law.umkc.edu/faculty/projects/ftrials/salem/salem.htm

* **Lincoln Assassination Theories**

  http://home.att.net/~rjnorton/Lincoln74.html

* **Saipan and the Mystery of Amelia Earhart**

  http://www.cnmi-guide.com/history/ww2/amelia/

* **National Geographic Kids Magazine: The Mystery Lives On**

  http://www.nationalgeographic.com/ngkids/9612/hart/

* **Virutal Exploration Society**

  http://www.unmuseum.org/earhart.htm

* **Naval History Magazine: The Earhart Mystery**

  http://www.usni.org/NavalHistory/Articles00/nhriley.htm

* **The Spanish American War (*the Maine*)**

  http://spanamwar.com

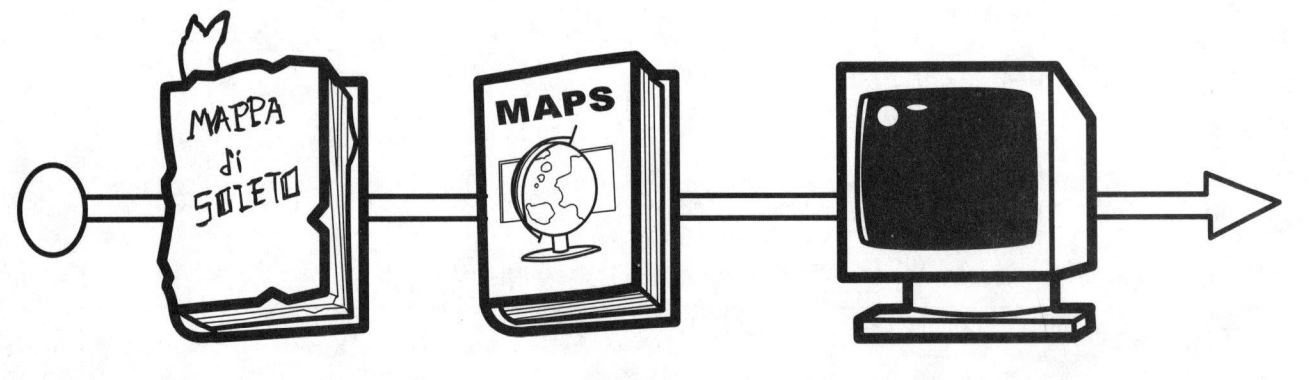